50% OFF

Online NYSTCE Multi-Subject: Teachers of Early Childhood Prep Course!

By Mometrix

Dear Customer,

We consider it an honor and a privilege that you chose our NYSTCE Study Guide. As a way of showing our appreciation and to help us better serve you, we are offering **50% off our online NYSTCE MS: Teachers of Early Childhood Course.** Many NYSTCE courses are needlessly expensive and don't deliver enough value. With our course, you get access to the best NYSTCE prep material, and **you only pay half price**.

We have structured our online course to perfectly complement your printed study guide. The NYSTCE Teachers of Early Childhood Online Course contains **in-depth lessons** that cover all the most important topics, **370+ video reviews** that explain difficult concepts, over **350 practice questions** to ensure you feel prepared, and more than **1,400 digital flashcards**, so you can study while you're on the go.

Online NYSTCE Teachers of Early Childhood Prep Course

Topics Include:

- Literacy and English Language Arts
- Mathematics
- Science and Technology
- Social Studies
- Fine Arts
- Health and Fitness
- Family and Consumer Science and Career Development

Course Features:

- NYSTCE Study Guide
  - Get content that complements our best-selling study guide.
- Full-Length Practice Tests
  - With over 350 practice questions, you can test yourself again and again.
- Mobile Friendly
  - If you need to study on the go, the course is easily accessible from your mobile device.
- NYSTCE Flashcards
  - Our course includes a flashcards mode with over 1,400 content cards for you to study.

To receive this discount, visit our website at mometrix.com/university/nystcetec or simply scan this QR code with your smartphone. At the checkout page, enter the discount code: **nytec50off**

If you have any questions or concerns, please contact us at support@mometrix.com.

NYSTCE

Multi-Subject: Teachers of Early Childhood (Birth-Grade 2) Practice Questions

Dear Future Exam Success Story

First of all, **THANK YOU** for purchasing Mometrix study materials!

Second, congratulations! You are one of the few determined test-takers who are committed to doing whatever it takes to excel on your exam. **You have come to the right place.** We developed these study materials with one goal in mind: to deliver you the information you need in a format that's concise and easy to use.

In addition to optimizing your guide for the content of the test, we've outlined our recommended steps for breaking down the preparation process into small, attainable goals so you can make sure you stay on track.

We've also analyzed the entire test-taking process, identifying the most common pitfalls and showing how you can overcome them and be ready for any curveball the test throws you.

Standardized testing is one of the biggest obstacles on your road to success, which only increases the importance of doing well in the high-pressure, high-stakes environment of test day. Your results on this test could have a significant impact on your future, and this guide provides the information and practical advice to help you achieve your full potential on test day.

Your success is our success

We would love to hear from you! If you would like to share the story of your exam success or if you have any questions or comments in regard to our products, please contact us at **800-673-8175** or **support@mometrix.com**.

Thanks again for your business and we wish you continued success!

Sincerely,
The Mometrix Test Preparation Team

Written and edited by the Mometrix Exam Secrets Test Prep Team
Printed in the United States of America

Table of Contents

Practice Test #1

Literacy and English Language Arts

1. A telecommunications salesman is writing informational text to persuade customers to agree to buy the products and services he is selling. One tactic includes advising the customer, "You are hemorrhaging money!" This is an example of which method of persuasion?

a. A generalization
b. Using a metaphor
c. Rhetorical question
d. Negative connotation

2. Which statement is most accurate about social contexts of L1 and L2 acquisition?

a. L2 learning can occur equally in varied contexts, from natural to educational, but L1 learning cannot.
b. L1s are only learned in natural contexts, while L2s are learned in educational contexts.
c. Variations in L2 proficiency can result from the different contexts of the learning of L2s.
d. L2s are never learned in natural contexts, as they are not the learners' natural languages.

3. What is the term for the final resolution of a fictional plot?

a. Exposition
b. Rising action
c. Falling action
d. Denouement

4. Which text(s) are likely to foster the greatest enthusiasm for reading and literature among students?

a. Free choice of reading texts, provided that students complete class assignments, projects, and discussions
b. An all-in-one textbook that includes all reading material for the year, study guides, and sample test questions
c. A variety of texts, including books, magazines, newspapers, stories from oral traditions, poetry, music, and films
d. A small selection of current best-selling books for children, some of which the children may already have read and liked

5. Learning to construct a reading response would be most beneficial in enhancing which language skill?

a. Oral presentation
b. Comprehension
c. Fluency
d. Learning a second language

6. The adaptation of language in a piece of writing to meet the author's purpose or audience is called:

a. Theme
b. Point of view
c. Style
d. Voice

7. In the three cueing systems model of word recognition in reading instruction, which of the following types of cues relates primarily to the structure of sentences and the arrangement of words?

a. Graphophonic
b. Semantic
c. Syntactic
d. Pragmatic

8. Which of the following processes used in writing is the most complex?

a. Evaluation
b. Application
c. Comprehension
d. Knowledge recall

9. Components of "explicit instruction" include:

a. Clarifying the goal, modeling strategies, and offering explanations geared to a student's level of understanding
b. Determining the goal, offering strategies, and asking questions designed to ascertain whether understanding has been reached
c. Reassessing the goal, developing strategies, and determining whether further reassessing of the goal is required
d. Objectifying the goal, assessing strategies, and offering explanations geared toward a student's level of understanding

10. *Carat, carrot, to, two,* and *too* share something in common. They are:

a. Nouns
b. Monosyllabic
c. Homophones
d. Diphthongs

11. A student identifies a text to read independently. According to an informal reading inventory the teacher just conducted, the student understands 48 percent of words in isolation that this text includes, reads words contained in this text with 90 percent accuracy in context, and correctly answers 68 percent of comprehension questions at this text's reading level. What does this indicate to the teacher?

a. This text is at the student's independent level; the teacher approves the student's selection.
b. This text is at the student's frustration level; the teacher helps the student find another text.
c. This text is at the student's instructional level, and the teacher approves it for guided reading.
d. This text is at some reading level that cannot be identified only from the student information.

12. Which of the following best explains the importance prior knowledge brings to the act of reading?

a. Prior knowledge is information the student gets through researching a topic prior to reading the text. A student who is well-prepared through such research is better able to decode a text and retain its meaning.
b. Prior knowledge is knowledge the student brings from previous life or learning experiences to the act of reading. It is not possible for a student to fully comprehend new knowledge without first integrating it with prior knowledge.
c. Prior knowledge is predictive. It motivates the student to look for contextual clues in the reading and predict what is likely to happen next.
d. Prior knowledge is not important to any degree to the act of reading, because every text is self-contained and therefore seamless. Prior knowledge is irrelevant in this application.

13. Which assessment will determine a student's ability to identify initial, medial, blended, final, segmented, and manipulated "units"?

a. Phonological awareness assessment
b. High-frequency word assessment
c. Reading fluency assessment
d. Comprehension quick-check

14. A teacher is working with a student who is struggling with reading. The teacher gives him a story with key words missing:

The boy wanted to take the dog for a walk. The boy opened the door. The ____ ran out. The ___ looked for the dog. When he found the dog, he was very _____.

The student is able to fill in the blanks by considering:

a. Syntax. Oftentimes, word order gives enough clues that a reader can predict what happens next.
b. Pretext. By previewing the story, the student can deduce the missing words.
c. Context. By considering the other words in the story, the student can determine the missing words.
d. Sequencing. By putting the ideas in logical order, the student can determine the missing words.

15. Which of the following statements is accurate according to research regarding students who are revising and rewriting?

a. Students only correct their mechanical errors in revisions.
b. Students often incorporate new ideas when they rewrite.
c. Students retain their original writing goals during revision.
d. Students' planning in prewriting is unaffected in rewriting.

16. Of the following, which statement is true about instruction in the alphabetic principle?

a. Letter-sound relationships with the highest utility should be the earliest ones introduced.
b. The instruction of letter-sound correspondences should always be done in word context.
c. Letter-sound relationship practice times should only be assigned apart from other lessons.
d. Letter-sound relationship practice should focus on new relationships, not go over old ones.

17. When a teacher instructs elementary school students in analyzing phonetically-regular words, which of the following would best represent a sequence from simpler to progressively more complex?

a. Long vowels, short vowels, consonant blends, CVC (consonant-vowel-consonant) and other common patterns, individual phonemes, blending phonemes, types of syllables, onsets and rimes
b. Onsets and rimes, short vowels, consonant blends, long vowels, blending phonemes, CVC and other common patterns, types of syllables, individual phonemes
c. Types of syllables, onsets and rimes, CVC and other common patterns, consonant blends, blending phonemes, individual phonemes, long vowels, short vowels
d. Individual phonemes, blending phonemes, onsets and rimes, short vowels, long vowels, consonant blends, CVC and other common patterns, types of syllables

18. Some of the students in Mr. Smith's fourth-grade class cannot decode words well enough to read fluently in class. He knows they are well behind grade level and that he needs to provide them with activities that will allow them to be successful, building skills and confidence at the same time. Which activity would be best for this purpose?

a. Enlist the parents' help by sending home a weekly list of sight words that the students can practice and memorize, decreasing the need to decode when they read.
b. Show the students how to create words out of movable alphabet tiles or magnetic letters, building (encoding) words as they sound them out.
c. Provide the children with early childhood readers that contain only very simple words so that the children will not feel badly as they read.
d. Allow those children having trouble to stop each time they reach a challenging word and sound it out carefully, recording it to a list that will be studied for homework.

19. Children develop phonological awareness:

a. Only through direct training given by adults
b. Only naturally, through exposure to language
c. Via both natural exposure and direct training
d. Via neither incidental exposure nor instruction

20. Regarding these elements of print awareness in literacy development, which is true?

a. All students with normal development can differentiate printed words from spaces.
b. To identify initial and final letters in words, students must identify words vs. spaces.
c. The only students not automatically knowing left-right directionality are certain ELLs.
d. Being able to identify basic punctuation is not important to reading comprehension.

21. A story about a young detective who solves mysteries using mental and physical skills would most likely be classified as which of the following?

a. Action and adventure
b. Historical fiction
c. Horror and ghost stories
d. Biography

22. Which of the following is the best use of technology in a language arts classroom?

a. Providing laptops to students to achieve more effective note-taking, access to word processing programs, and access to the internet
b. Encouraging the use of slide shows or similar programs to support lectures and oral presentations, as well as to organize pertinent class concepts
c. Incorporating a computer-based "language lab" in which students can listen to texts and engage in interactive word-study and comprehension activities
d. Whenever possible, watching film interpretations based on texts studied in class

23. A teacher is teaching students using rime analogies to support reading comprehension. Which of the following skills best relates to the use of rime analogies?

a. Students will be able to identify and use metaphors and similes.
b. Students will be able to identify and use similar sounding words.
c. Students will be able to identify and use similarly spelled words.
d. Students will be able to identify and use figures of speech.

24. Which of the following choices represents the smallest unit of language that possesses semantic meaning?

a. Morpheme
b. Grapheme
c. Phoneme
d. Word stem

25. Which of these is a strategy most applicable to evaluating a young student's reading comprehension of narrative writing?

a. Whether the student can retell a story that s/he has just read
b. Whether the student can decode unfamiliar words in the story
c. Whether the student can invent spellings for unfamiliar words
d. Whether the student can identify and produce rhyming words

26. Third-grade students typically receive their spelling word lists each Monday so that they can practice them at home before the test on Friday. While their teacher is pleased that the students usually receive high grades on spelling tests, she observes that they misspell those same words when writing in journals or doing classwork. How should this teacher modify her instruction?

a. Post a list of vocabulary words when the students are writing to help them recall correct spellings.
b. Integrate spelling words into writing, reading, grammar, phonics, and other activities to help students learn the words in a variety of contexts.
c. Provide more time, such as a two-week period, between tests so that students have more time to study.
d. Review the words before certain activities to increase immediate recall of correct spellings.

27. Which adult would be most effective in helping a student who frequently mispronounces sounds both in reading and in conversation?

a. A whole language specialist
b. A speech pathologist
c. A paraprofessional
d. A psychologist

Refer to the following for question 28:

A class considers the paragraph below:

Sarah and Kelly grinned at one another conspiratorially as they approached Dad, who was quietly reading his paper in the living room. "Dad, we'd like to ride our bikes down to Emil's house today," giggled Kelly. She glanced at her sister and shifted her weight from foot to foot. Dad appeared to think this over for a moment and replied, "Sure, that's fine with me!" The girls scampered to get their bikes and were soon on their way. With the children gone, Dad noticed how peaceful and quiet the house sounded. His reverie was quickly interrupted as he heard Mom calling from upstairs, "okay, everybody, I told you at breakfast that I need as much help as I can get to help me give the dog a bath, clean the house and finish the laundry today!" Dad groaned, knowing that he had been conned!

28. Which method would be best for helping students determine the meaning of the word "reverie" in the next to last sentence?

a. Using context clues
b. Making an educated guess
c. Decoding the prefix, root, and suffix of the word
d. Previewing and reviewing

29. Assonance means that two or more words

a. Start with the same sound
b. End with the same sound
c. Have the same vowel sound
d. Sound like an item they portray

30. The perspective from which a story is told is called:

a. Theme
b. Point of view
c. Style
d. Voice

31. Early in the school year, all members of a group of kindergarten students are able to chant the alphabet. The teacher is now teaching the students what the alphabet looks like in written form. The teacher points to a letter, and the students vocalize the corresponding sound. Alternatively, the teacher vocalizes a phoneme and a student points to it on the alphabet chart. The teacher is using _____________ in her instruction.

a. letter–sound correspondence
b. rote memorization
c. predictive analysis
d. segmentation

32. The following sentence is which of the following sentence types?

The questions in this test can give you an idea of what kinds of questions you might find on the actual test; however, they are not duplicates of the actual test questions, which cover the same subject material but may differ in form and content.

a. Simple
b. Complex
c. Compound
d. Compound-complex

33. A teacher is working with a group of third graders at the same reading level. Her goal is to improve reading fluency. She asks each child in turn to read a page from a book about mammal young. She asks the children to read with expression. She also reminds them they don't need to stop between each word; they should read as quickly as they comfortably can. She cautions them, however, not to read so quickly that they leave out or misread a word. The teacher knows the components of reading fluency are:

a. Speed, drama, and comprehension
b. Cohesion, rate, and prosody
c. Understanding, rate, and prosody
d. Rate, accuracy, and prosody

34. Among four categories of media that teachers instruct students to identify, in which one are books primarily classified?

a. Media used in one-on-one communication
b. Media used for entertainment
c. Media to inform many people
d. Media for persuading people

35. Which of the following statements adheres to Information Literacy Standards?

a. Students accessing information must critically evaluate it and its sources before using it.
b. Students accessing information should ascertain how much of it they need after they find it.
c. Students accessing information efficiently sacrifice incidental learning.
d. Students accessing information must avoid using it for purposes it was not meant to serve.

36. Which of the following is true regarding children's reading fluency?

a. The lack of reading fluency is always due to word-decoding deficits.
b. Children's motivation to read is unaffected by their reading fluency.
c. Some children need only more reading practice to develop fluency.
d. Fluency has equal impact on school performance at all grade levels.

37. To help students understand abstract concepts in the print materials they read, which instructional aids that teachers provide can students always use three-dimensionally?

a. Examples
b. Manipulatives
c. Graphic organizers
d. Charts, tables, graphs

38. If a child appears delayed in speech development, which of the following is the best course to follow?

a. Take a wait-and-see approach, as there are wide variations in patterns of speech development
b. Use in-depth evaluations and early intervention to assist the child with language delays
c. Help the child with common developmental speech problems, such as saying "w" for "r"
d. Have the child repeat common words and phrases after an adult pronounces them

39. A fourth-grade teacher had her students write haiku in order to promote the students' _________.

a. reading comprehension
b. vocabulary
c. word identification skills
d. confidence

40. Of the following, which represents an indirect way in which students receive instruction in and learn vocabulary?

a. Being exposed repeatedly to vocabulary in multiple teaching contexts
b. Being exposed to vocabulary when adults read aloud to them
c. Being pre-taught specific words found in text prior to reading
d. Being taught vocabulary words over extended periods of time

41. Using the information from the following exhibits and your pedagogical knowledge related to literacy and English language arts, write a response of approximately 400-600 words in which you:

- Discuss one strength and one area for improvement exhibited by the student related to language and literacy development
- Identify one instructional strategy, approach, or activity that could be applied to support the student's strengths and learning needs
- Explain why the instructional strategy, approach, or activity you identified would be appropriate and effective for this purpose
- Support your reasoning with specific examples from the exhibits and your pedagogical knowledge and skills related to English language arts and literacy development

Be sure to support your response with specific examples from all three exhibits.

EXHIBIT 1

TEACHER NOTES

Student: Madelynn **Age:** 7 **Grade:** 2

Home Language: English **IEP?:** No

10/1: I met Madelynn's mom at open-house last night and she gave me some insight into Madelynn's interests. She said that getting Madelynn to read at home is a struggle because she often becomes frustrated and bored. Her mother did say that Madelynn sometimes enjoys reading nonfiction books, particularly about animals.

10/4: Today I conducted oral reading fluency screenings for fall. Madelynn's rate is 40 WCPM, which is eleven less than the fall 50th percentile benchmark of 51 WCPM with an accuracy rate of 90%. She seemed unfocused and tried to read as quickly as possible without paying much attention to accuracy. Several times, she trailed off and began to mumble as she read, and it became difficult to understand her. She demonstrated significant gaps in overall comprehension and had difficulty pronouncing some multisyllabic words.

10/6: Today students gave oral presentations on self-selected reading books. Madelynn chose a nonfiction book about reptiles and gave a fantastic presentation. She recalled several details about reptiles and explained key facts about them very well. Madelynn was clearly interested in the topic. This presentation went much better than her last one after reading an assigned fictional book.

10/10: To introduce a social studies unit on landforms, students independently read an informational passage and completed corresponding activities. The passage was lengthier than the class was used to, and although Madelynn typically prefers nonfiction, she appeared visibly overwhelmed and frustrated. Several times, I noticed her staring off into the distance and had to redirect her attention. She did not complete the reading assignment in the twenty minutes allotted.

Exhibit 2

Reading Literature

The teacher administers an oral reading assessment and records their performance to determine their oral reading fluency. After having them read aloud a grade-level passage, the teacher asks corresponding comprehension questions. Madelynn's performance record is shown below, followed by a transcript of the conversation between Madelynn and the teacher about the text.

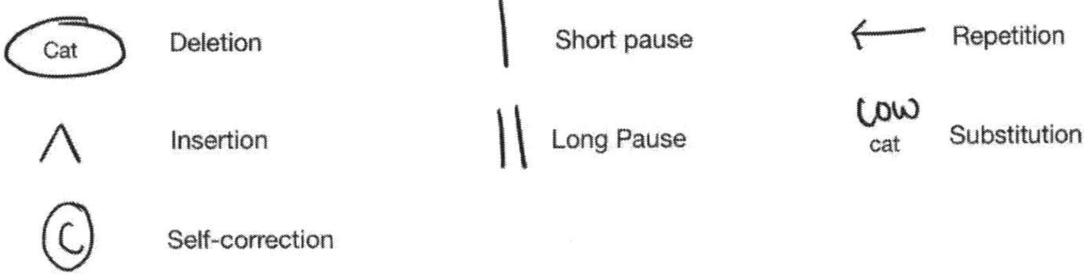

READING PASSAGE

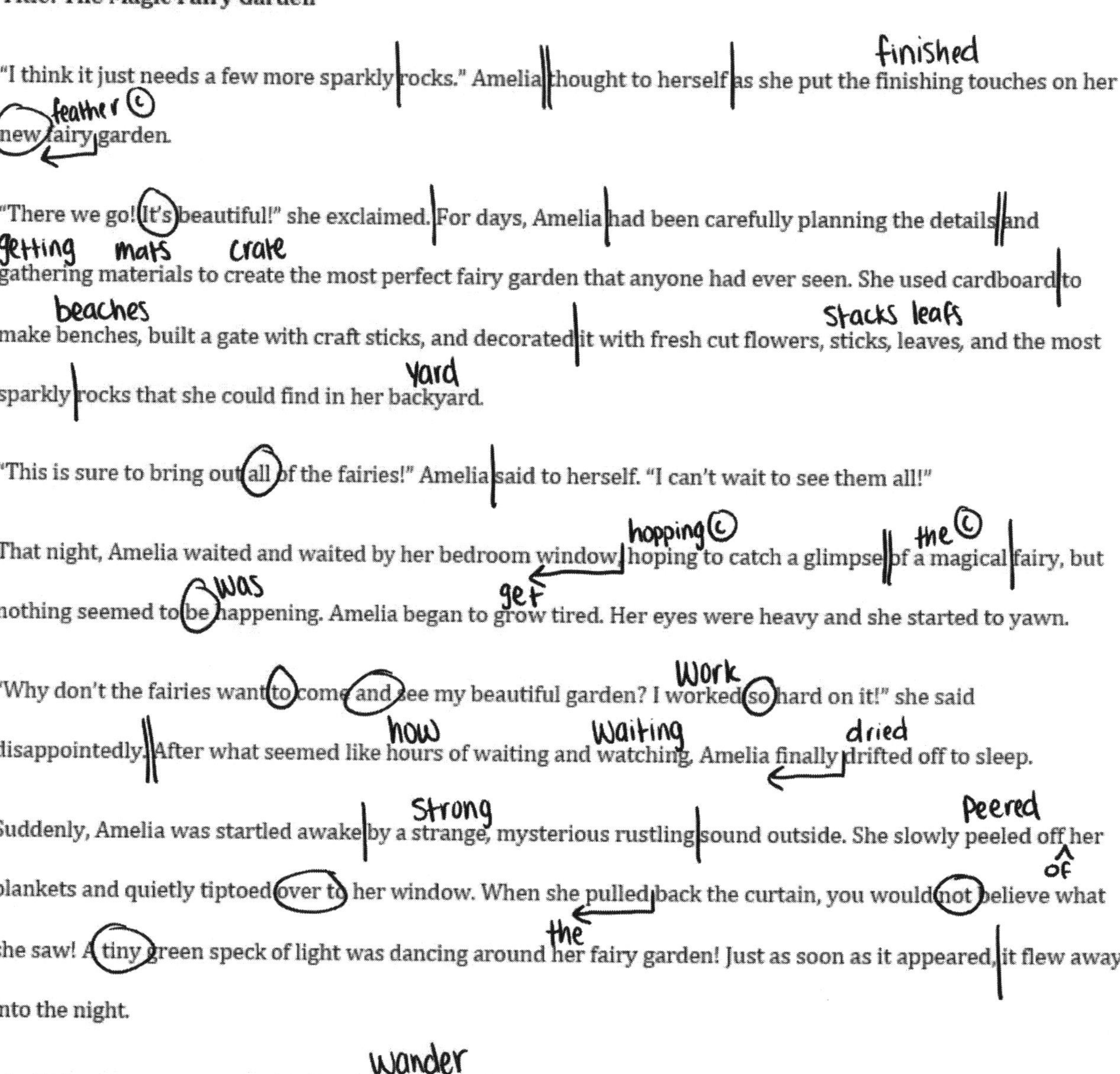

Title: The Magic Fairy Garden

"I think it just needs a few more sparkly rocks." Amelia thought to herself as she put the finishing touches on her new fairy garden.

"There we go! It's beautiful!" she exclaimed. For days, Amelia had been carefully planning the details and gathering materials to create the most perfect fairy garden that anyone had ever seen. She used cardboard to make benches, built a gate with craft sticks, and decorated it with fresh cut flowers, sticks, leaves, and the most sparkly rocks that she could find in her backyard.

"This is sure to bring out all of the fairies!" Amelia said to herself. "I can't wait to see them all!"

That night, Amelia waited and waited by her bedroom window, hoping to catch a glimpse of a magical fairy, but nothing seemed to be happening. Amelia began to grow tired. Her eyes were heavy and she started to yawn.

"Why don't the fairies want to come and see my beautiful garden? I worked so hard on it!" she said disappointedly. After what seemed like hours of waiting and watching, Amelia finally drifted off to sleep.

Suddenly, Amelia was startled awake by a strange, mysterious rustling sound outside. She slowly peeled off her blankets and quietly tiptoed over to her window. When she pulled back the curtain, you would not believe what she saw! A tiny green speck of light was dancing around her fairy garden! Just as soon as it appeared, it flew away into the night.

"Could that have been a fairy?", Amelia wondered.

After Madelynn reads the passage aloud, the teacher asks some comprehension questions to determine her level of understanding about what he has read. Below is a transcript of their conversation.

Teacher: What was the title of this story?

Madelynn: I can't remember the whole thing. The....something about a garden I think.

Teacher: Do you think this story was fiction or nonfiction?

Madelynn: It's probably made-up.

Teacher: Who was the main character of this story?

Madelynn: A little girl named Emily...I mean...Amy. No, Amelia!

Teacher: Good! What was Amelia doing in the story?

Madelynn: Making a garden.

Teacher: Where did the story take place?

Madelynn: Probably outside.

Teacher: What makes you think so?

Madelynn: Because that's where people usually make gardens.

Teacher: Do you remember what kind of garden she was making?

Madelynn: One that she made with a bunch of different stuff.

Teacher: Who did she want to come visit the garden?

Madelynn: Let me think...(*long pause*)...oh yeah! Fairies, right?

Teacher: Yes! Did they visit her?

Madelynn: Yep!

Teacher: What sort of items did Amelia put in her garden?

Madelynn: I can't really remember that. Maybe she planted some seeds. Or a tree. I would probably want to plant seeds in a garden.

Teacher: What was the problem Amelia had in the story?

Madelynn: It took a long time to decorate. And then she fell asleep.

Teacher: Do you remember how the story ended?

Madelynn: I only just remember that she was sleeping.

Exhibit 3

Reading Informational Text

After a slide show presentation on various landforms, the teacher gives each student an informational reading along with a matching activity and corresponding comprehension questions for students to answer in their reader response journals. Students are asked to read the passage independently. The text, matching activity, comprehension questions, and Madelynn's responses appear below.

Reading Passage

What you see when you look outside depends on the geography of where you live. **Geography** is the study of the physical and living things on Earth. This simple definition includes many things, including the landforms that make up the Earth's surface. **Landforms** are the natural physical features that we find when we go outside. Different regions of Earth have different kinds of landforms. Some examples of landforms we might find are deserts, plains, mountains, oceans, lakes, rivers, islands, or peninsulas.

Deserts are very dry, hot, and arid areas of land. Very little rain falls in deserts during the year, and because of that, there is very little water. You will not find a lot of vegetation in deserts, either, and only certain kinds of animals can live there. Even though deserts are quite hot during the day, they get very cold at night.

Plains are large, flat areas of land and can be found on all seven continents. Many plains are grassy, but they can also be deserts or forests. **Mountains** can also be found on every continent. These large landforms stretch high above the ground and can be very steep and rocky. Mountains are usually formed over millions of years by pressure created between tectonic plates.

Areas of land that are surrounded by water on all sides are called **islands**. Islands can be found in almost any large body of water, such as oceans, rivers, or even lakes. Many islands are big enough for people to live on them, and some are even their own countries! Some areas of land are only surrounded by water on three sides. These are called **peninsulas**.

Bodies of water are also landforms. The **ocean** is the largest body of salt water on Earth and makes up 98% of all the water on the planet. All other bodies of water eventually lead to the ocean. We have five names for different regions of the ocean. They are called the Atlantic, Pacific, Indian, Arctic, and Antarctic.

Rivers are bodies of fresh water that flow into other bodies of water, such as the ocean. They can be wide or narrow, shallow or deep, and are constantly moving. Rivers are used by people for many purposes, such as fishing, transporting goods, or even drinking! **Lakes** are another type of freshwater body. These bodies of water are surrounded by land and can either be natural or man-made.

MATCHING ACTIVITY:

Directions: Match each landform with the correct description.

Landform	Student Choices	Answer Choices
River	**a.**	a. Surrounded completely by water
Peninsula	**f.**	b. Hot, dry, arid area of land
Island	**a.**	c. Largest body of salt water on Earth
Mountain	**h.**	d. Body of water surrounded by land
Lake	**e.**	e. Constantly flowing body of fresh water
Ocean	**c.**	f. Large, flat area of land
Plain	**b.**	g. Land surrounded by water on three sides
Desert	**f.**	h. Tall, steep, rocky landform

Comprehension Questions:

1. What is the definition of landforms?
2. What are the two types of freshwater bodies found on Earth?
3. What do we call different regions of the Earth's Ocean?
4. What are some ways that people use rivers?
5. What are two characteristics of deserts?
6. How are mountains usually formed?

Madelynn's Responses:

1. The difnishin of land forms is antyhing we can find on the land
2. Ocens and also rivirs
3. We can call them ether salt water or frish water
4. Mayb for a boat or to ketch fishes
5. Desrts are awlays hot out
6. By mayb wen a vulkano rupts

Mathematics

1. If $f(x) = \frac{x^3-2x+1}{3x}$, what is $f(2)$?

a. $\frac{1}{3}$
b. $\frac{1}{2}$
c. $\frac{5}{6}$
d. $\frac{5}{2}$

2. Which of the following represents the net of a triangular prism?

a. 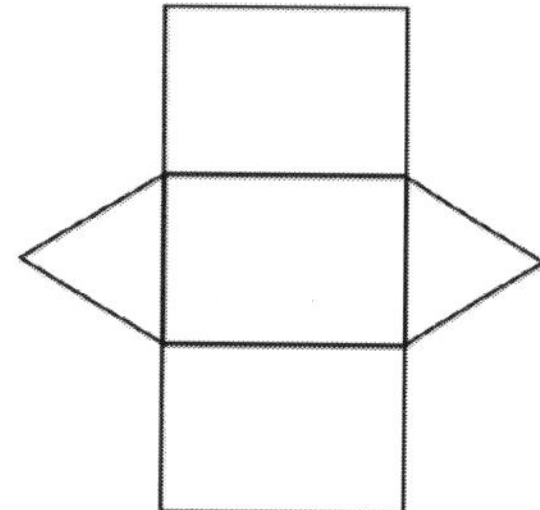

b. 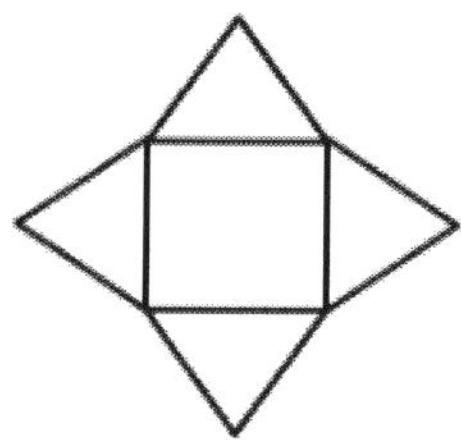

c. 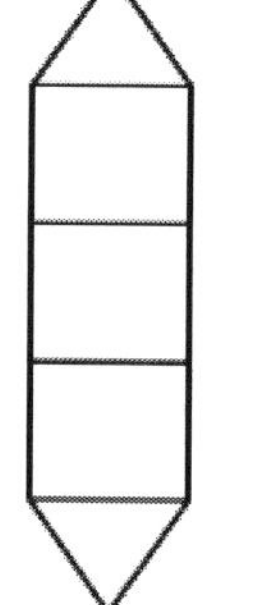

d. 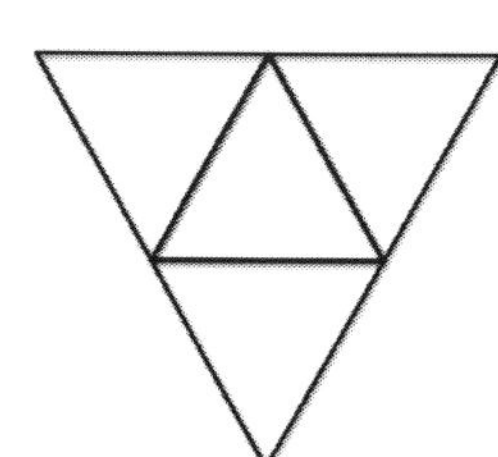

3. Andrew rolls a die. What is the probability he gets a 4 or an even number?

a. $\frac{1}{4}$
b. $\frac{1}{2}$
c. $\frac{2}{3}$
d. $\frac{3}{4}$

4. Kyra sets aside $\frac{1}{3}$ of her income to pay rent and utilities at her apartment. If the monthly cost of rent and utilities is $1,050, what is her monthly salary?

a. $3,150
b. $3,225
c. $3,750
d. $4,050

5. On a floor plan drawn at a scale of 1 : 100, the area of a rectangular room is 30 cm². What is the actual area of the room?

a. 30,000 cm^2
b. 300 m^2
c. 3,000 m^2
d. 30 m^2

6. Katrina wants to solve this math problem: "If there are 30 days in a month and today is the 12th, how many days until the end of the month?" What should be her first problem-solving step?

a. Devise a plan for solving the problem
b. Carry out the plan she created
c. Look back to check that her answer is correct
d. Understand what the problem is asking

7. Mrs. Jennings has 8 packs of stickers. Each pack contains 12 pages, and each page contains 20 stickers. Write a mathematical expression that describes the total number stickers. Based on the student work below, which students have misconceptions regarding the correct way to mathematically express the scenario.

Megan	Julio	Craig	Samantha
$8(12 \times 20)$	28×12	$12 \times 20 \times 8$	$8 + 12 + 20$

a. Julio and Samantha
b. Julio and Megan
c. Craig and Samantha
d. Julio and Craig

8. Solve the system of equations.

$$3x + 4y = 2$$
$$2x + 6y = -2$$

a. $\left(0, \frac{1}{2}\right)$
b. $\left(\frac{2}{5}, \frac{1}{5}\right)$
c. $(2, -1)$
d. $\left(-1, \frac{5}{4}\right)$

9. Which of the following numbers is a multiple of 23?

a. 39
b. 48
c. 101
d. 92

10. Ms. Elliott asks her fifth-grade students, "Do you prefer chocolate or vanilla ice cream?" If the probability of her students preferring chocolate ice cream is 0.6, what is the probability of her students preferring vanilla ice cream?

a. 0.6
b. 0.4
c. 0.3
d. 0.5

11. McKenzie shades $\frac{1}{5}$ of a piece of paper. Then, she shades an additional area $\frac{1}{5}$ the size of what she just shaded. Next, she shades another area $\frac{1}{5}$ as large as the previous one. As she continues the process to infinity, what is the limit of the shaded fraction of the paper?

a. $\frac{1}{5}$
b. $\frac{1}{4}$
c. $\frac{1}{3}$
d. $\frac{1}{2}$

12. Claus has \$20 to spend at the local fair. The entrance fee is \$2.50, and tickets for the booths are \$2 each. Which of the following inequalities represents the number of tickets x that Claus can afford with his \$20?

a. $2.50x + 2x \leq 20$
b. $2.50 + 2x \leq 20$
c. $2x \leq 20 + 2.50$
d. $2.50 + 2x \geq 20x$

13. The 6th grade teachers at Washington Elementary School are doing a collaborative unit on cherry trees. Miss Wilson's math classes are making histograms summarizing the heights of black cherry trees located at a local fruit orchard. How many of the trees at this local orchard are 73 feet tall?

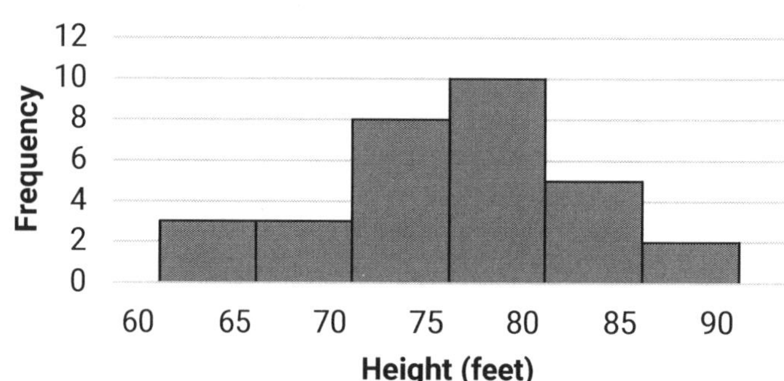

a. 8
b. That information cannot be obtained from this graph
c. 9
d. 17

14. While teaching the concept of addition, a first-grade teacher gives each student two dice to use as manipulatives. Which of the following types of representation is this teacher using to communicate this concept?

a. Concrete
b. Verbal
c. Graphic
d. Pictorial

15. For any natural numbers, a, b, and c, assume $a < b$ and $a < c$. Which of the following statements is NOT necessarily true?

a. $b < c$
b. $a < \frac{b+c}{2}$
c. $a < bc$
d. $2a < bc$

16. Kevin saves \$3 during Month 1. During each subsequent month, he plans to save 4 more dollars than he saved during the previous month. Which of the following equations represents the amount he will save during the nth month?

a. $a_n = 3n - 1$
b. $a_n = 3n + 4$
c. $a_n = 4n + 3$
d. $a_n = 4n - 1$

17. Ms. Chen is instructing her students on divisibility rules. Which of the following rules can be used to determine if a number is divisible by 6?

a. The last digit of the number is divisible by 2 or 3.
b. The number ends in 6.
c. The number is divisible by 2 and 3.
d. The last two digits of the number are divisible by 6.

18. Marcus is mowing yards and doing odd jobs to earn money for a new video game system that costs \$325. Marcus only charges \$6.50 per hour. Which of the following equations represents the number of hours Marcus needs to work to earn \$325?

a. $6.50x = 325$
b. $6.50 + x = 325$
c. $325x = 6.50$
d. $6.50x + 325 = x$

19. For any natural numbers, a, b, and c, assume $a|b$ and $a|c$. Which of the following statements is NOT necessarily true?

a. $b|c$
b. $a|(b - c)$
c. $a|bc$
d. $a|(b + c)$

20. Mr. Ray is teaching a lesson about place value. He is trying to describe the relationship between the two 8s in the number 203.988.

Which choices provide an accurate way to describe the relationship between the two 8s in the number 203.988?

a. "The 8 in the hundreds place is ten times larger than the 8 in the thousands place."
b. "The 8 in the hundredths place is ten times larger than the 8 in the thousandths place."
c. "The 8 in the thousands place is ten times larger than the 8 in the hundreds place."
d. "The 8 in the thousandths place is ten times smaller than the 8 in the hundredths place."

21. Which graph represents the linear equation $y = 2x - 3$?

a.

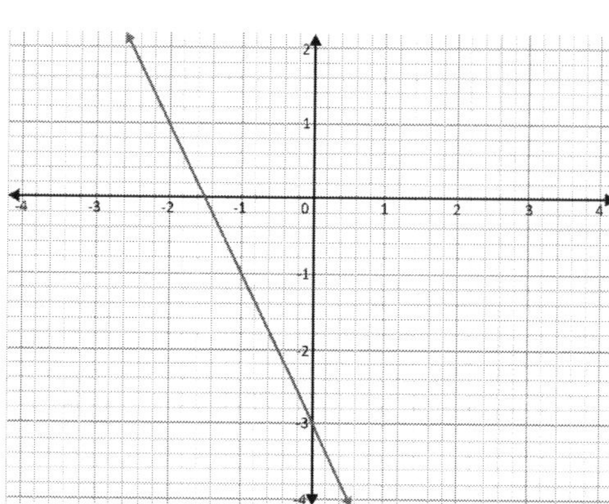

c.

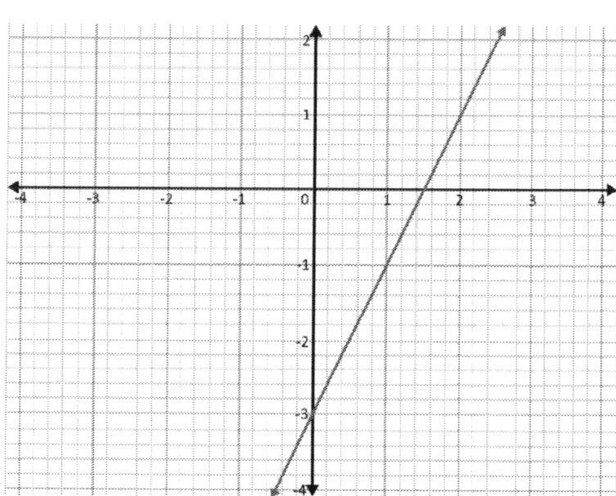

b.

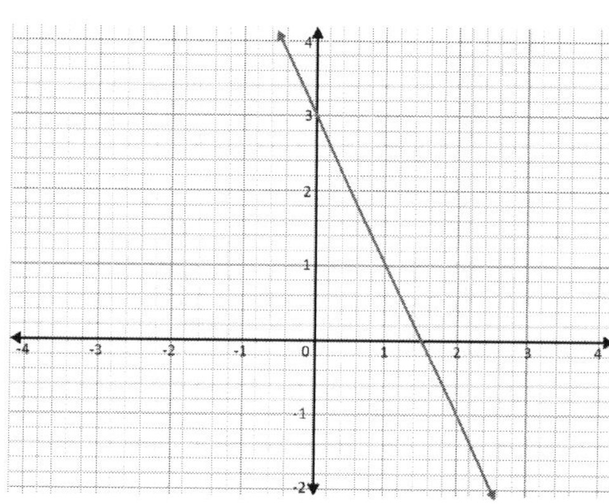

d.

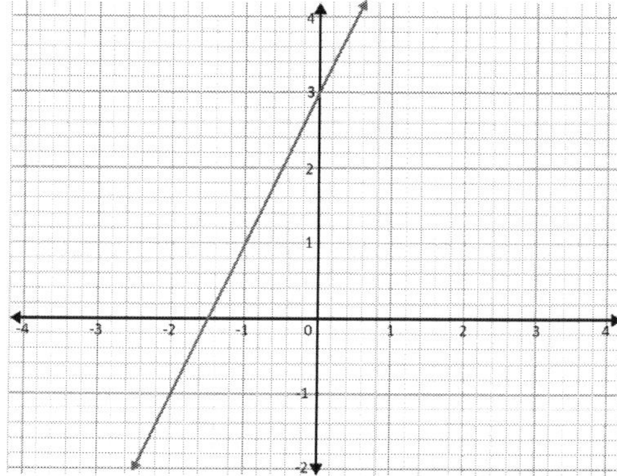

22. The variables x and y have a linear relationship. The table below shows a few sample values. Which of the following graphs correctly represents the linear equation relating x and y?

x	y
−2	−11
−1	−8
0	−5
1	−2
2	1

a. 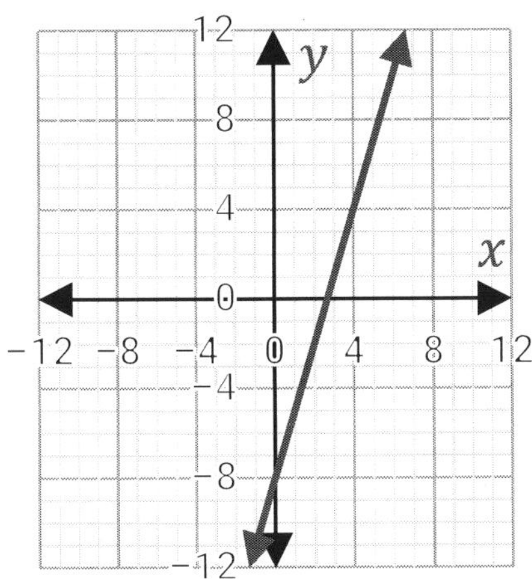

b. 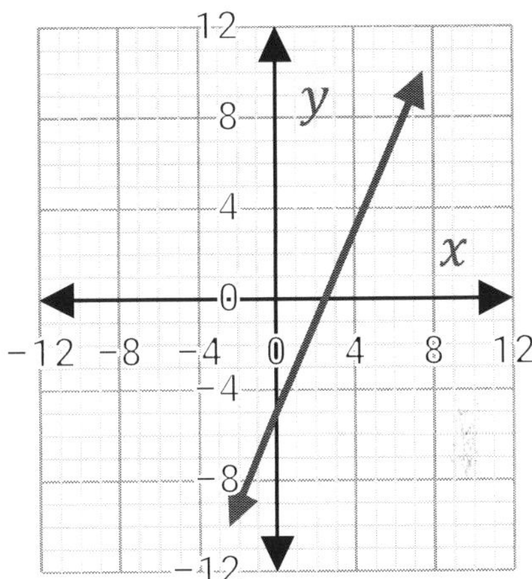

c. 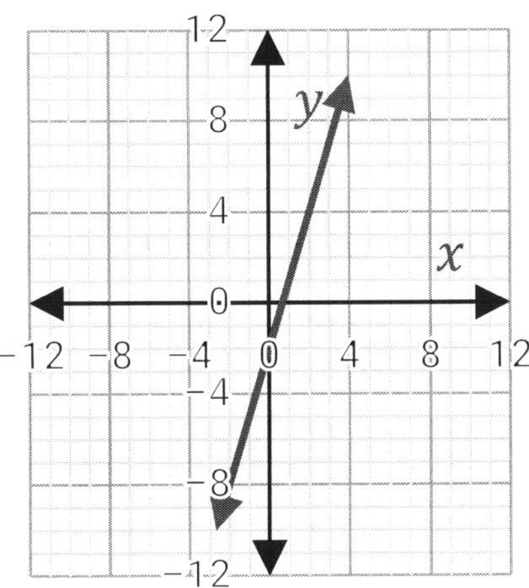

d. 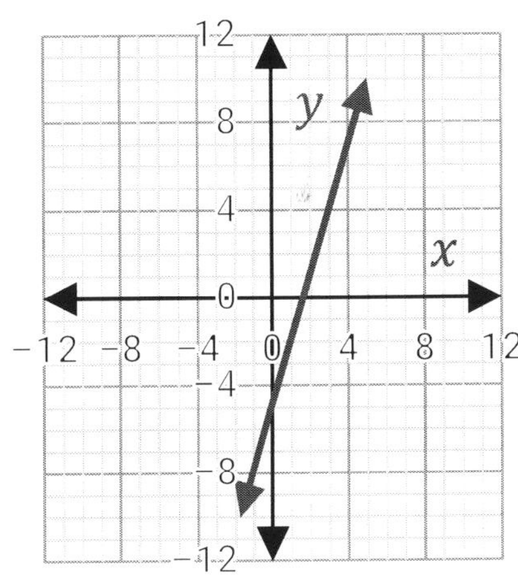

23. Which of the following goals is appropriate in the category of algebraic reasoning for first-grade students?

a. Students represent one- and two-step problems involving addition and subtraction of whole numbers to 1,000 using pictorial models, number lines, and equations.
b. Students represent real-world relationships using number pairs in a table and verbal descriptions.
c. Students represent word problems involving addition and subtraction of whole numbers up to 20 using concrete and pictorial models and number sentences.
d. Students recite numbers up to at least 100 by ones and tens beginning with any given number.

24. In a class of 24 students, 18 completed their projects on time. What fraction of the students failed to complete their projects on time?

a. 1/4
b. 2/3
c. 3/4
d. 5/8

25. What is the correct solution for x in the following system of equations?

$$\begin{cases} x - 1 = y \\ y + 3 = 7 \end{cases}$$

a. $x = 6$
b. $x = 5$
c. $x = 4$
d. $x = 8$

26. Identify the cross-section polygon formed by a plane containing the given points on the cube.

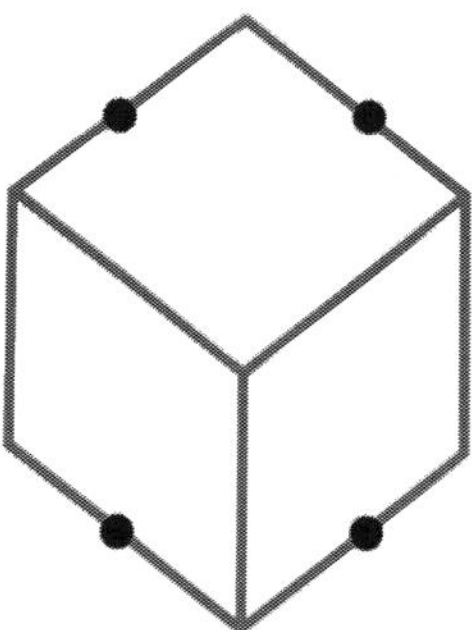

a. Rectangle
b. Trapezoid
c. Pentagon
d. Hexagon

27. Ann must walk from Point A to Point B and then to Point C. Finally, she will walk back to Point A. If each unit represents 5 miles, which of the following BEST represents the total distance she will have walked?

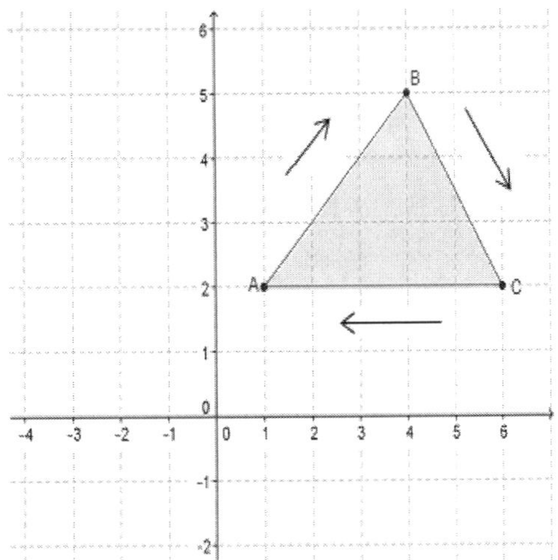

a. 42 miles
b. 48 miles
c. 56 miles
d. 64 miles

28. Which of the following is NOT a way to teach young children to recognize patterns?

a. Count by twos beginning with 5
b. Comparing geometric shapes
c. Solving for x in an equation
d. Analyzing the results of a class survey

29. Which of the following descriptions best fits a hexagonal prism?

a. 8 faces, 18 edges, 12 vertices
b. 6 faces, 18 edges, 12 vertices
c. 8 faces, 16 edges, 8 vertices
d. 6 faces, 14 edges, 10 vertices

30. Which of the following expressions is equivalent to $-3x(x-2)^2$?

a. $-3x^3 + 6x^2 - 12x$
b. $-3x^3 - 12x^2 + 12x$
c. $-3x^2 + 6x$
d. $-3x^3 + 12x^2 - 12x$

31. A coin is tossed 300 times. How many of those tosses can you expect to show heads?

a. 50
b. 100
c. 150
d. 200

32. Yu is paid every 2 weeks and sets aside $60 from every paycheck to save for a car. How much does he have in his car fund after a year (count as 52 weeks)?

a. $1,560
b. $1,525
c. $1,490
d. $1,450

33. Which of the following statements is (are) true when $f(x) = \frac{x^2-2x-3}{x^3+3x^2-6x-8}$?

I. The graph $f(x)$ has two vertical asymptotes at $x = 2$ and $x = -4$.
II. The x- and y-intercepts of the graph of $f(x)$ are both 3.

a. I
b. II
c. I and II
d. Neither statement is true.

34. A teacher is assessing the students' understanding of the appropriate units for length, area, and volume. Which of the following only lists units of area?

a. $\text{in}^2, \text{mm}^2, \text{ft}^2$
b. $\text{yd}, \text{yd}^2, \text{yd}^3$
c. mm, cm, m
d. $\text{m}^2, \text{s}^2, \text{km}^2$

35. Two companies offer monthly cell phone plans, both of which include free text messaging. Company A charges a $25 monthly fee plus five cents per minute of phone conversation, while Company B charges a $50 monthly fee and offers unlimited calling. At what total duration of monthly calls do both companies charge the same amount?

a. 500 hours
b. 8 hours and 33 minutes
c. 8 hours and 20 minutes
d. 5 hours

36. Which of the following is an example of the commutative property?

a. $8 + 12 = 12 + 8$
b. $20 + 0 = 20$
c. $9(3 + 6) = 9 \times 3 + 9 \times 6$
d. $2 + (-2) = 0$

37. A tree with a height of 15 feet casts a shadow that is 5 feet in length. A man standing at the base of the shadow formed by the tree is 6 feet tall. How long is the shadow cast by the man?

a. 1.5 feet
b. 2 feet
c. 2.5 feet
d. 3 feet

38. Nikki buys a used book that is marked down 35% from the original price. She pays 8.25% sales tax. Her total cost is $9.14. What was the original price of the book?

a. $11.99
b. $12.49
c. $12.99
d. $13.49

39. $2(7+8)^2 - 12(6 \times 2) =$

a. 119
b. 225
c. 306
d. 604

40. In order to analyze the real estate market for two different zip codes within the city, a realtor examines the most recent 100 home sales in each zip code. She considered a house which sold within the first month of its listing to have a market time of one month; likewise, she considered a house to have a market time of two months if it sold after having been on the market for one month but by the end of the second month. Using this definition of market time, she determined the frequency of sales by the number of months on the market. The results are displayed below. Which of the following is a true statement for these data?

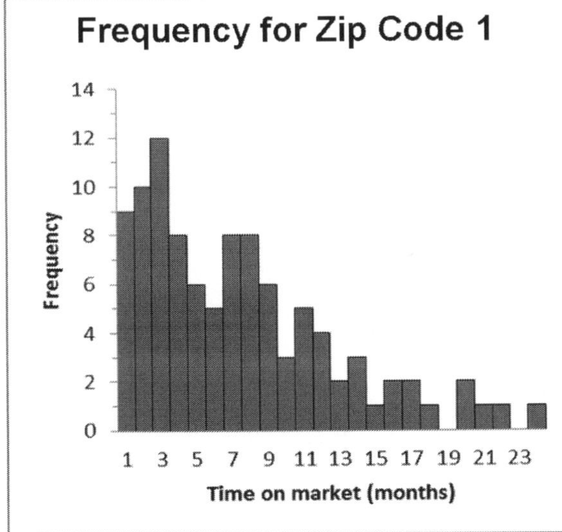

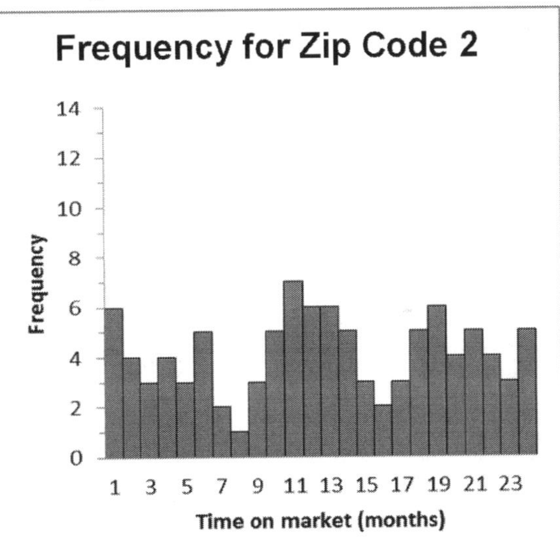

a. The median time a house spends on the market in Zip Code 1 is five months less than Zip Code 2
b. On average, a house spent seven months longer on the market in Zip Code 2 than in Zip Code 1.
c. The mode time on the market is higher for Zip Code 1 than for Zip Code 2.
d. The median time on the market is less than the mean time on the market for Zip Code 1.

41. Using the information from the following exhibits and your pedagogical knowledge related to mathematics, write a response of approximately 400-600 words in which you:

- Discuss one strength and one area for improvement exhibited by the student related to mathematics
- Identify one instructional strategy, approach, or activity that could be applied to support the student's strengths and learning needs
- Explain why the instructional strategy, approach, or activity you identified would be appropriate and effective for this purpose
- Support your reasoning with specific examples from the exhibits and your pedagogical knowledge and skills related to mathematics

Be sure to support your response with specific examples from all three exhibits.

Exhibit 1

Background Information

Students in a kindergarten classroom have been learning number names and the count sequence. They are familiar with rote counting to 100 by ones and skip counting to 100 by tens. Now, the class will begin working on counting to tell the number of objects. In this lesson, students will be working on the following standard:

Counting and Cardinality (NY-K.CC) - Count to tell the number of objects

Understand the relationship between numbers and quantities up to 20; connect counting to cardinality

Answer counting questions using as many as 20 objects arranged in a line, a rectangular array, and a circle. Answer counting questions using as many as 10 objects in a scattered configuration.

Given a number from 1-20, count that many objects.

Specifically, the teacher has planned instruction to build students' understanding of one-to-one correspondence. The lesson will include activities to promote the concepts that the last number name said tells the number of objects counted, successive number names refer to quantities that are one larger, as well as students' ability to count a given number of objects.

Exhibit 2

Description of Class Activity

The teacher will review rote counting with students using a number chart. Then, the teacher will use direct instruction to introduce the concept of one-to-one correspondence by displaying several examples with visual representations of various numbers.

Students will independently practice these concepts using number cards and dot markers. Each card either asks students to count a given number of objects or represent a particular number using their dot marker. Examples of such cards appear below.

As students work, the teacher will walk around the room to monitor student progress and evaluate overall understanding.

Directions: Count the number of objects in each row	**Name______________**
1. 	
2. 	
3. 	
4. 	
5. 	

Directions: Use your dot markers to represent each number below.	**Name______________**
8	
11	
6	
9	
14	

Exhibit 3

Excerpt of a Conversation with a Student

As students work, the teacher formatively assesses student understanding by monitoring progress, asking questions about their process, and asking questions to extend learning. An excerpt of one such interaction with a student along with samples of the student's work appears below.

Directions: Count the number of objects in each row	Name Ben
1. ⬬⬬⬬⬬⬬⬬	ᘓ
2. ★★★	Ɛ
3. ▲▲▲▲▲▲▲▲▲	9
4. ■■■■■	S
5. ♥♥♥♥♥♥♥♥ ♥♥♥♥♥♥	12

Directions: Use your dot markers to represent each number below.	Name Ben
8	
11	
6	
9	
14	

Teacher: I see you got all of the answers in your first card correct, Ben. Good job! Can you count the first one aloud for me?

Ben: One, two, three, four, five, six!

Teacher: Great! Now I'm going to draw two more ovals next to these. How many ovals do we have now?

Ben: One, two, three, four, five, six, seven, eight. Eight ovals!

Teacher: Good! In the second one, we have three stars. I'm going to draw three more next to them. Can you try counting on from three to see how many we have now?

Ben: Um...three...just a second.

The teacher notices Ben using his finger to silently recount the stars.

Ben: Now there are six.

Teacher: That's right. Now, let's take a look at your second card. It looks like you got some of these correct as well! Can you tell me what you did?

Ben: It was easy! I just dotted and counted at the same time!

Teacher: Let's take a look at number two in your second card. Can we try to count your dots one more time?

Ben: Let's see...one, two, three, four, five, six, seven, eight, nine, um...hang on, I need to start over.

Arts and Sciences

1. Which of the following is not one of the primary elements of art?

a. Dimension
b. Unity
c. Texture
d. Space

2. Of the following, who was NOT a dispatch rider notifying Americans of British troop movements reported by American surveillance in 1775?

a. Paul Revere
b. William Dawes
c. John Parker
d. Samuel Prescott

3. Which of the following BEST describes the significance of the US Supreme Court's decision in the Dred Scott case?

a. The ruling effectively declared slavery to be a violation of the Constitution.
b. The ruling guaranteed full citizenship rights to freed slaves.
c. The ruling turned many Southerners against the Supreme Court.
d. The ruling furthered the gap between North and South and hastened the Civil War.

4. Which of the following activities would be MOST appropriate for helping students develop an appreciation for the value and role of art in US society?

a. Having students create a slide show presentation about a famous American artist
b. Asking students to create a timeline showing when famous works of American art were created
c. Taking students on a field trip to an art museum
d. Asking students to write an essay comparing and contrasting the influence that two famous American artists or artworks had on US society

5. The Seven Years' War, called the French and Indian War by the Colonists:

a. Was the precursor to the American Revolution
b. Was a conflict related to European colonization
c. Primarily took place in Canada
d. Ended European conquests

6. The physical geography of a region most directly affects which of the following?

a. The religious beliefs of the native population
b. The family structure of the native population
c. The dietary preferences of the native population
d. The language spoken by the native population

7. Which of the following represents a chemical change?

a. Water sublimating
b. An apple turning brown
c. Salt dissolving in water
d. Rock being pulverized

8. Which of the following statements correctly compares rocks and minerals?

a. Minerals may contain traces of organic compounds, while rocks do not.
b. Rocks are classified by their formation and the minerals they contain, while minerals are classified by their chemical composition and physical properties.
c. Both rocks and minerals can be polymorphs.
d. Both rocks and minerals may contain mineraloids.

9. Which part of a hurricane features the strongest winds and greatest rainfall?

a. Eye wall
b. Front
c. Eye
d. Outward spiral

10. How are igneous rocks formed?

a. Years of sediment are laid down on top of each other and forced together.
b. Acid rain caused by pollution creates holes in metamorphic rocks.
c. Dust and pebbles are pressed together underground from Earth's heat and pressure.
d. Magma from a volcanic eruption cools and hardens.

11. What are the first ten amendments to the Constitution more commonly known as?

a. The Civil Rights Act
b. Common law
c. The Equal Protection clause
d. The Bill of Rights

12. Which of the following kinds of activities are BEST suited for developing perceptual-motor skills in adolescents?

a. One-step physical activities to build foundational skills
b. Fun physical activities that consist of identifiable steps
c. Any physical activities at all, as long as they are fun
d. Any activities that involve hearing, seeing, or touching

13. In order for a pigment to reach the desired consistency for fluid painting, with which of the following should it NOT be combined?

a. Turpentine
b. Fresco
c. A tempera
d. An oil medium

14. What does the 10th Amendment establish?

a. Any power not given to the federal government belongs to the states or the people.
b. The president is responsible for executing and enforcing laws created by Congress.
c. Congress has the authority to declare war.
d. The Supreme Court has the authority to interpret the Constitution.

15. The price of oil drops dramatically, saving soda pop manufacturers great amounts of money spent on making soda pop and delivering their product to market. Prices for soda pop, however, stay the same. This is an example of what?

a. Sticky prices
b. Indiscriminate costs
c. Stable demand
d. Aggregate expenditure

16. The philosophy of the late 17th-18th centuries that influenced the Constitution was from the Age of:

a. Enlightenment
b. Empire
c. Discovery
d. Industry

17. Thomas Jefferson embraced a theological philosophy called deism, which promotes which of the following?

a. Abolition
b. Atheism
c. Separation of church and state
d. A theocratic central government

18. Two companion models, gradualism and punctuated equilibrium, dominate evolutionary theory. Which of the following statements is most consistent with the theory of punctuated equilibrium?

a. Fossils show changes over large periods of time.
b. Fossils showing intermediate characteristics may not necessarily be found.
c. Speciation occurs gradually.
d. Evolution is a slow, steady process.

19. Most federal judges have served as local judges, lawyers, and law professors. These are ________ qualifications.

a. Formal
b. Required
c. Informal
d. Recommended

20. Fossils are least likely to be found in which type of rock?

a. Sedimentary rock
b. Metamorphic rock
c. Igneous rock
d. Fossils are commonly found in all types of rock

21. Social and behavioral theories of learning stress the importance of

a. Good behavior on the part of students
b. The social interactions of students that aid or inhibit learning
c. A reward system for good behavior or growth in skills
d. The direct connection between thoughts and speech

22. What portion of the federal budget is dedicated to transportation, education, national resources, the environment, and international affairs?

a. Mandatory spending
b. Discretionary spending
c. Undistributed offsetting receipts
d. Official budget outlays

23. Which of the following tempos is played between 120 and 168 beats per minute?

a. Presto
b. Moderato
c. Allegro
d. Largo

24. Which of the following is an example of chemical weathering?

a. Rain freezing on the roadway
b. Ivy growing on the side of a wooden house
c. Vinegar fizzing when poured on a rock
d. A river carrying sediment downstream

25. What type of compound is formed by the combination of two or more nonmetallic elements with one another?

a. Organic
b. Ionic
c. Covalent
d. Chemical

26. What did the Mason-Dixon Line divide?

a. The East from the West before the western states were incorporated
b. The East from the West along the Mississippi River
c. The North from the South before the Civil War
d. The Senate from the House of Representatives

27. Which of the following is NOT true of a chemical reaction?

a. Matter is neither gained nor lost.
b. Heat is absorbed or released.
c. The rate of the reaction increases with temperature.
d. The products have a different number of atoms than the reactants.

28. A pulley lifts a 10-kg object 10 m into the air in 5 minutes. Using this information, you can calculate which of the following?

a. Mechanical advantage
b. Efficiency
c. Frictional resistance
d. Power

29. What steps should precede drawing a conclusion about a hypothesis?

a. Testing, observing, and recording data
b. Communicating the hypothesis to others
c. Comparing data with data of other groups
d. Reporting the results so they can be replicated

30. What happens to the temperature of a substance as it is changing phase from a liquid to a solid?

a. Its temperature increases due to the absorption of latent heat.
b. Its temperature decreases due to the heat of vaporization.
c. Its temperature decreases due to the latent heat of fusion.
d. Its temperature remains the same due to the latent heat of fusion.

31. When the Senate held an impeachment hearing against Andrew Johnson for overstepping his authority, what did they invoke?

a. Checks and balances
b. Bicameralism
c. Legislative oversight
d. Supremacy

32. How are animals of the Mollusca phylum able to respire?

a. Through gills
b. Through a trachea
c. Through lungs
d. Through muscle contraction

33. Which of the following is true regarding the Tropic of Capricorn?

a. It separates the northern and southern hemispheres.
b. It separates the eastern and western hemispheres.
c. It is the southernmost latitude at which the sun can appear directly overhead at noon.
d. It is the northernmost latitude at which the sun can appear directly overhead at noon.

34. Which of the following is an example of a descriptive study?

a. Comparing the average height of male vs female penguins of a particular species
b. Investigating the growth rate of fungi in various synthetic media
c. Testing the effectiveness of a drug with a double-blind study
d. Split-testing the impact on sales of a new description of menu items.

35. Which of the following statements is NOT an accurate statement about the Puritans in England?

a. The Puritans unconditionally gave all their support to the English Reformation.
b. The Puritans saw the Church of England as too much like the Catholic Church.
c. The Puritans became a chief political power because of the English Civil War.
d. The Puritans' clergy mainly departed from the Church of England after 1662.

36. What happens to gas particles as temperature increases?

a. The average kinetic energy decreases while the intermolecular forces increase.
b. The average kinetic energy increases while the intermolecular forces decrease.
c. Both the average kinetic energy and the intermolecular forces decrease.
d. Both the average kinetic energy and the intermolecular forces increase.

37. Which of the following learning goals is most appropriate for a second-grade unit on personal financial literacy?

a. The students will be able to calculate how money saved can accumulate into a larger amount over time.
b. The students will be able to balance a simple budget.
c. The students will be able to identify the costs and benefits of planned and unplanned spending decisions.
d. The students will be able to define money earned as income.

38. Which of the following composers is MOST strongly associated with the Romantic Period?

a. Johann Sebastian Bach
b. Maurice Ravel
c. Aaron Copland
d. Johannes Brahms

39. Which geographic features were most conducive to the development of early civilizations?

a. Rivers
b. Deserts
c. Forests
d. Mountains

40. The following represents a simple food chain. What trophic level contains the greatest amount of energy?

tree → caterpillar → frog → snake → hawk → worm

a. Tree
b. Caterpillar
c. Hawk
d. Worm

Answer Key and Explanations

Literacy and English Language Arts

1. B: This is an example of a metaphor. The literal meaning of hemorrhaging is copious bleeding. In this example it is used figuratively in a metaphor for losing money at a volume and rate comparable to severe blood loss denoted by hemorrhage. It is not a generalization. An example of using a generalization persuasively is "We all want peace, not war." It is not a rhetorical question or a question at all. An example of using a rhetorical question (needing no answer) persuasively is "Wouldn't you rather get paid more than less?" The example is not of negative connotation, because the word "hemorrhage" already has a negative denotation—in other words, the literal meaning of hemorrhaging is never a good thing. An example of using negative word connotation persuasively is, "You could stay with this *expensive* plan..." followed by contrasting positive connotation: "...or choose the *money-saving* plan I'm offering."

2. C: Second languages can be learned in a number of educational contexts. For example, they can be segregated from the L1, formally taught via the medium of the L1, taught through submersion, or taught within the language classroom but not used to communicate outside of it. The L2 can also be learned in several natural contexts. Because of these variations, L2 learners may acquire different elements of the language or may vary in how much of the language they acquire, so choice C is correct. Just like an L2, an L1 can also be learned in an education or natural context, so choice A is incorrect. While many L1s are learned naturally at first, they are learned in educational contexts as well, so choice B is incorrect. Just like L1s, L2s can be learned and used naturally, so choice D is incorrect.

3. D: The denouement is the end of a story. The other choices are intermediate steps in writing a story.

4. C: Students can easily become bored or disinterested in reading if they are not exposed to a variety of reading texts. Also, reading can be overwhelming or frustrating for students who are still learning to read fluently or to comprehend what they read. By incorporating media, oral stories, and various types of print, students of all ability levels can build both fluency and comprehension skills. This approach also enables the teacher and students to discuss the relationship between all aspects of literacy—including speaking, listening, thinking, viewing, and reading.

5. B: Reading responses can take various forms. The most common form of reading response is likely to be targeted student writing. Students may use journals, worksheets, or other formats to construct written responses to something they have read. The purpose of this type of assignment can range from fostering an appreciation of written text to helping a student prepare for an activity in class. Students may also engage in creating an oral reading response in the form of a presentation or debate. Ultimately, reading response increases a student's capacity to understand what is read and to analyze personal responses to the text.

6. C: An author writing a humorous book will use a different style than an author writing a biography.

7. C: In the three cueing systems model used in teaching reading, there are three types of cues that allow readers to comprehend texts: syntactic cues, phonological or graphophonic cues, and semantic cues. Syntactic cues, those provided by syntax, exist in the grammar of the text, and include cues such as sentence structure, word order, parts of speech, and inflections or endings.

Therefore, choice C is correct. Choices A and B refer to other cueing systems, so these choices are incorrect. The phonological or graphophonic cueing system (A) is a set of cues that exist in the language's speech sounds, or phonemes, and the letters representing them. The semantic cueing system (B) is a set of cues that exist in the meanings of words and the morphemes that make up words. Choice D is incorrect because pragmatic cues are not one of the three sets of cues included in the three cueing system model. Pragmatic cues involve reader understanding of their reasons for reading and of how text structures operate. (In linguistics, pragmatics is the study of how language is used for social communication.)

8. A: Choice A is correct as evaluation (i.e., making critical judgments about some information) commonly incorporates the processes that the other answer choices refer to and is therefore more complex than they are. Application (B) requires taking information learned and using it in new or different circumstances. Comprehension (C) requires showing understanding of the information learned. Knowledge recall (D) involves showing proficiency in information learned.

9. A: Explicit instruction involves clarifying the goal, modeling strategies, and offering explanations geared to a student's level of understanding. Explicit instruction is well organized and structured. It offers easily understood steps and depends in part on frequent reference to previously learned materials.

10. C: Homophones are words that are pronounced the same but differ in meaning. For example, a bride wears a 2-carat ring, but a horse eats a carrot. These words are not all nouns or monosyllabic, and none of them are dipthongs. Dipthongs (D) are a single-syllable sound made up by combining two vowels, such as in the words *weird*, *applause*, and *boy*.

11. B: One set of criteria suggested for use with informal reading inventories (Pumfrey, 1976) equates the independent reading level to knowing 95-100 percent of words in isolation, 99-100 percent accuracy reading words in context, and answering comprehension questions 90-100 percent correctly; the instructional level to knowing 60-94 percent of words in isolation, 95-98 percent accuracy reading words in context, and answering comprehension questions 70-89 percent correctly; and the frustration level with knowing below 50 percent of words in isolation, reading below 95 percent of words accurately in context, and answering below 70 percent of comprehension questions correctly. Hence, the text described is at the student's frustration level and too difficult.

12. B: Prior knowledge, which rises from experience and previous learning, provides a framework by which new knowledge gained from the act of reading can be integrated. Every act of reading enriches a student's store of prior knowledge and increases that student's future ability to comprehend more fully any new knowledge acquired through reading.

13. A: The words in this question prompt are most often used to refer to *sounds* made while reading. Initial/onset, medial, and final sounds are decoded in the beginning, middle, and end of words. When a teacher needs to assess an emergent or struggling reader's ability to differentiate between sounds in words, he or she may use a phonological awareness assessment. This tool will provide the teacher with information about the student's current ability to decode or encode words.

14. C: By considering the other words in the story, the student can determine the missing words. The student is depending on the information supplied by the rest of the story. This information puts the story into context.

15. B: Researchers have found that the writing process both forms a hierarchy and is observably recursive. Moreover, they find that when students continually revise their writing, they are able to consider new ideas and to incorporate these ideas into their work. Therefore, choice B is correct. Students who are rewriting and revising do not merely correct mechanical errors (A); they also add to the content and quality of their writing. Furthermore, research shows that writers (including students) not only revise their actual writing during rewrites, but they also reconsider their original writing goals rather than always retaining them (C), and they revisit their prewriting plans rather than leaving these unaffected (D).

16. A: While there is no consensus among experts as to any universal sequence of instruction for teaching the alphabetic principle through phonics instruction, they do agree that, to enable children to start reading words as soon as possible, the highest-utility relationships should be introduced earliest. For example, the letters *m, a, p, t,* and *s* are all used frequently, whereas the *x* in *box*, the sound of *ey* in *they*, and the letter *a* when pronounced as it is in *want* have lower-utility letter-sound correspondences. Important considerations for the alphabetic principle are to teach letter-sound correspondences in isolation, not in word contexts; to teach them explicitly; to give students opportunities to practice letter-sound relationships within their other daily lessons, not only separately; and to include cumulative reviews of relationships taught earlier along with new ones in practice opportunities.

17. D: To instruct students in word analysis following a sequence progressing from simpler to more complex, teachers would first introduce individual phonemes (speech sounds); then the blending of two or more individual phonemes; then onsets and rimes (i.e., phonograms and word families) such as *-ack*, *-ide*, *-ay*, *-ight*, *-ine*, etc.; then the easier short vowels, followed by the more difficult long vowels; then blends of individual consonants; then CVC (consonant-vowel-consonant) words (e.g., *bag, hot, red, sit*) and other common patterns of consonants and vowels in words; and then the six most common types of syllables (i.e., closed, VCe, open, vowel team, *r*-controlled, and C-*le*).

18. B: This prompt focuses not only on reading fluency skills, but also on the issue of the young reader's confidence. It is very common for students who feel unsuccessful at reading to avoid the skill altogether. The teacher in this question realizes something important: it is vital to build a student's confidence with reading as he or she builds skill. In choice A there is a faulty assumption that a student could ever memorize enough words to eliminate the need to decode. While some students with processing disorders or different learning styles do rely more heavily on sight words, this practice should not be solely relied upon. In choice C the students will likely feel negatively about being asked to read young children's books; their lack of confidence may be reinforced by this plan. In choice D students may also be frustrated by the extra work they are required to do without any evidence of success with this practice. In choice B, students can build their fluency skills by creating words with various sounds, which is often easier for students than decoding as they are learning to read. As their knowledge of letter-sound relationships grows, they will become better at decoding words they see on the page. Allowing students to encode will also provide them with more chances to feel successful as they learn.

19. C: Children develop phonological awareness through a combination of incidental learning via being naturally exposed to language in their environments, and receiving direct instruction from adults. They do not develop it solely through one or the other, or neither.

20. B: Students must be able to distinguish between printed words and the spaces between them to identify the first and last letters of each word, as spaces are the boundaries between words. It is not true that all normally developing students can tell words from spaces: those not exposed to or familiar with print media may need to be taught this distinction. Although left-to-right directionality is more of a problem for ELL students whose L1s have different writing or printing directions (e.g., some Asian languages are written vertically, some can be written vertically or horizontally, and some Semitic languages like Hebrew and Arabic are written right-to-left), again, children unfamiliar with print or writing may also not know writing, print, or book directionality either. Identifying basic punctuation is important to reading comprehension as it affects meaning. For example, consider "Let's eat, Grandma" vs. "Let's eat Grandma"—one comma differentiates an invitation to dinner from a cannibalistic proposal.

21. A: Action and adventure stories do not rely on magical or supernatural events as do fantasy, horror, and ghost stories. They are not biographical unless telling the life of a real person.

22. C: There is currently a wide variety of technology resources available that can support class instruction. However, teachers must choose carefully in order to ensure that the technology is useful and relevant to the intended learning outcomes for the class. The language lab described allows students to experience text through both listening and reading, thereby utilizing different processes in the brain. The interactive modules also support decoding and comprehension skills that go along with the texts. This use of technology reinforces important skills in a way that will be unique and interesting for the students.

23. C: Analogizing is based on recognizing the pattern of letters in words that share phonological and orthographical similarities. In phonology and in spelling, the initial sound of a word is called an *onset*, whereas the sounds that follow the onset are called the *rime*. The following words each have a different onset sound, but share the same rime: *rent*, *sent*, *bent*, and *dent*. Rime analogies are an explicit teaching method that helps draw attention to patterns in rime and onset spellings. As students become more familiar with these patterns, they should be able to decode common rime patterns in words faster and with greater accuracy, contributing to higher reading fluency.

24. A: A phoneme is a unit of language that represents the smallest unit of sound. For instance, the *k* in *kit* or the *ph* in *graph* both represent English phonemes. Graphemes are written phonemes and can be alphabetic letters, numbers, characters, punctuation marks, and so on. Neither phonemes nor graphemes have semantic meaning unless they are used as part of a larger unit of language, such as the morpheme. Morphemes can be roots, prefixes, and suffixes. The word *rechargeable* is comprised of three morphemes: *re*, *charge*, and *able*. Each component of this word has a meaning unto itself, but when combined with the others, each one is used to make a new word with a new meaning.

25. A: Narrative writing is storytelling, as opposed to expository or informational writing. Ability to retell the story is a key strategy for assessing a student's reading comprehension. Decoding new words (B), inventing original spellings for new words (C), and identifying and producing rhymes (D) are all abilities whereby teachers can assess student skills for decoding printed words, but not their comprehension of printed text.

26. B: Spelling is often taught in a systematic way. Students receive words and memorize them for quizzes and tests. However, spelling is related to many aspects of language and must be treated as a dynamic subject. Integrating the words into other parts of language instruction will help students not only learn how to spell correctly, but also to recall meanings of words and various rules of English spelling and grammar. By using the same words in different subjects, the students will retain the information more readily than if they study the words intensely for one week in only one context.

27. B: There are many different adults who can assist children in acquiring various types of language. If a child inconsistently mispronounces certain sounds in reading, he or she may simply need a reminder or instruction from a teacher. Often, children will not acquire knowledge of certain letters or sounds until a certain age. However, the child in this scenario mispronounces words consistently both in reading and in conversation. This combination suggests that the child is not physically able to make certain speech sounds. A speech-language pathologist can assist in determining whether or not the child's mispronunciations indicate the need for therapy. A speech pathologist can also work directly with the child to help him or her learn how to make certain sounds.

28. A: The text at hand contains several clues as to the meaning of this word, including the use of the words "peaceful" and "quiet" in the preceding sentence. Students may also recognize that Mom's requests for help with undesirable household chores interrupted Dad's peaceful, quiet 'reverie." Choice "a" is the specific method that would be most appropriate for determining the word's meaning; Choice "b" is a less reliable or systematic way of doing the same thing. Choice "c" would not be helpful in this case since "reverie" is not a word that can be decoded in a traditional manner. Choice "d" would not offer a realistic solution to this question since previewing and reviewing are more helpful in increasing comprehension of informative texts, rather than vocabulary words.

29. C: Words with assonance have the same vowel sound. An example would be cow and loud.

30. B: The point of view is generally first- or third-person. Stories in the second person exist, but these are rare.

31. A: Letter–sound correspondence relies on the relationship between a spoken sound or group of sounds and the letters conventionally used in English to write them.

32. D: This is an example of a compound-complex sentence, so choice D is correct. The other choices are incorrect, as they refer to different sentence types. A simple (A) sentence contains no more than one independent clause (i.e., a subject and a finite verb) and no dependent clauses. Its subject and verb may be compound (e.g., "John and Mary" as the subject, or "comes and goes" as the verb). A complex (B) sentence contains an independent clause and one or more dependent clauses. Dependent clauses are joined to independent clauses or other dependent clauses by subordinating conjunctions (as in "after she left") or relative pronouns (as in "that he had never heard"). A compound (C) sentence contains two or more independent clauses. The compound-complex sentence, as its name implies, combines both compound and complex sentence structures. It combines more than one independent clause with at least one dependent clause. In the example sentence given, the first two clauses, joined by "however," are independent, and the clause modifying "actual test questions," beginning with "which cover," is a relative, dependent clause.

33. D: Fluent readers are able to read smoothly and comfortably at a steady pace (rate). The more quickly a child reads, the greater the chance of leaving out a word or substituting one word for another (for example, *sink* instead of *shrink*). Fluent readers are able to maintain accuracy without sacrificing rate. Fluent readers also stress important words in a text, group words into rhythmic phrases, and read with intonation (prosody).

34. C: When teaching students about various media types, the four categories listed as choices are ways to classify them. One-on-one communication media includes emails, phone calls, and letters but not books. Entertainment media includes movies, TV shows, and video games; novels are included, but not the wider class of books. (Note that there are many more kinds of books than novels.) Informative media includes books, newspapers, websites, and radio news broadcasts. Persuasive media includes advertising, direct mail marketing, telemarketing calls, and infomercials.

35. A: It is a standard of Information Literacy that students must use their own critical thinking skills to evaluate the quality of the information and its sources before they use it, so choice A is correct. Another standard of Information Literacy is that the student should ascertain how much information he or she needs before seeking out the information, as identifying what information is necessary after uncovering excessive information is inefficient (B). An additional Information Literacy standard is to access necessary information in an efficient and effective way. However, none of these standards include the idea that students will sacrifice any incidental learning by being efficient in their accessing of information, so choice C is incorrect. Another part of Information Literacy Standards is the principle that students should use the information they find in ways that are effective for their specific purposes; this does not require that students avoid using information for purposes that it was not meant to serve, so choice D is incorrect.

36. C: While *some* children's reading lacks fluency due to deficits in their word-decoding abilities, this is not *always* (A) the case: some children simply need more reading practice to develop fluency. Children's motivation to read (B) *is* affected by their reading fluency: when reading is laborious, children do not enjoy it and avoid reading; when reading is easy, children enjoy it and want to read. Fluency has much *greater* impact (D) on the performance of students in higher grades, when the volume of reading required of them in school is exponentially greater.

37. B: Manipulatives are three-dimensional concrete objects that students can not only look at but also manipulate, as the name indicates (e.g., touch, move, rearrange, dismantle, reassemble). Examples may be three-dimensional objects, demonstrations, or (more often) verbal descriptions given orally, printed, or written. Graphic organizers are diagrams (e.g., Venn diagrams), charts, timelines, concept maps, word webs, etc., which are two-dimensional, visual, graphic materials. Charts, tables, and graphs, though less pictorial and conceptual and more linear and numerical than graphic organizers, are also two-dimensional in print, online, or on screen.

38. B: Use in-depth evaluation and early intervention to assist the child with language delays. Research shows that early intervention is highly successful, while a wait-and-see approach just prolongs the delayed language development. Common developmental problems like saying "w" instead of "r" disappear on their own as the child matures and do not need intervention.

39. B: Writing haikus will promote students' vocabularies. The tightly controlled syllabic requirements will cause students to search for words outside their normal vocabularies that will fit the rigid framework and still express the writer's intended meanings. Often, students will rediscover a word whose meaning they know, but they don't often use.

40. B: Indirect ways in which students receive instruction and learn vocabulary include through daily conversations, reading on their own, and being read aloud to by adults. Direct instruction and learning in vocabulary include teachers providing extended instruction exposing students repeatedly to vocabulary words in multiple teaching contexts, teachers pre-teaching specific words found in text prior to students reading it, and teachers instructing students over extended time periods and having them actively work with vocabulary words.

41. Scoring Rubric:

Constructed response items will be scored holistically on a scale of 1-4 according to the following performance indicators:

Completion	The degree to which the candidate addresses all parts of the prompt
Organization/Clarity	The degree to which the candidate presents their response and supporting evidence in an organized, coherent manner
Accuracy/Relevancy	The degree to which the candidate demonstrates meaningful and accurate knowledge and skills pertaining to the prompt
Use of supporting evidence	The degree to which the candidate uses specific, appropriate, and relevant examples and reasoning from the exhibits provided

Candidates that receive an overall score of "4" demonstrate excellent pedagogical knowledge and skills related to the prompt.

- All parts of the prompt are addressed with thoroughness and attention to detail
- Information in the response is very well-organized, clear, and accessible to the reader
- The response demonstrates accurate and relevant pedagogical knowledge and skills relative to all items in the prompt
- The response includes ample specific, appropriate, and relevant examples from the exhibits provided with detailed explanations

Mathematics

1. C: Substitute 2 for each x and simplify.

$$f(2) = \frac{(2)^3 - 2(2) + 1}{3(2)} = \frac{8 - 4 + 1}{6} = \frac{5}{6}$$

2. A: The net of a triangular prism has three rectangular faces and two triangular faces, and the rectangular faces must all be able to connect to each other directly.

3. B: Since they are not mutually exclusive events, $P(4 \text{ or } E) = P(4) + P(E) - P(4 \text{ and } E)$. Substituting the probability of each event gives $P(4 \text{ or } E) = \frac{1}{6} + \frac{1}{2} - \frac{1}{6} = \frac{1}{2}$.

4. A: Kyra's monthly salary may be modeled as $\frac{1}{3}x = 1{,}050$. Multiplying both sides of the equation by 3 gives $x = 3{,}150$.

5. D: Since there are 100 cm in a meter, on a 1 : 100 scale drawing, each centimeter represents one meter. Therefore, an area of one square centimeter on the drawing represents one square meter in actuality. Since the area of the room in the scale drawing is 30 cm^2, the room's actual area is 30 m^2.

Another way to determine the area of the room is to write and solve an equation, such as this one: $\frac{l}{100} \times \frac{w}{100} = 30 \text{ cm}^2$, where l and w are the dimensions of the actual room.

$$\frac{lw}{10{,}000} = 30 \text{ cm}^2$$

$$\text{Area} = 300{,}000 \text{ cm}^2$$

Since this is not one of the answer choices, convert cm^2 to m^2.

$$300{,}000 \text{ cm}^2 \times \frac{1 \text{ m}}{100 \text{ cm}} \times \frac{1 \text{ m}}{100 \text{ cm}} = 30 \text{ m}^2$$

6. D: Before you can solve a problem, you must decide what it is asking.

7. A: Mrs. Jennings has 8 sticker packs containing 12 pages each. 8 groups of 12 can be represented as 8×12, or $8(12)$. Each of these pages contains 20 stickers. This means that the product of 8 and 12 should be multiplied by 20. Correct answers include $8(12 \times 20)$ and $12 \times 20 \times 8$. Julio and Samantha have incorrect answers. Julio appears to have the misconception that $8 + 20 = 28$ and 28×12 is the same thing as $8 \times 20 \times 12$. Samantha appears to have the misconception that the sum of 8, 12, and 20 is the same thing as the product of 8, 12, and 20.

8. C: A system of linear equations can be solved by using matrices or by using the graphing, substitution, or elimination (also called linear combination) method. The elimination method is shown here:

$$\begin{aligned} 3x + 4y &= 2 \\ 2x + 6y &= -2 \end{aligned}$$

In order to eliminate x by linear combination, multiply the top equation by 2 and the bottom equation by –3 so that the coefficients of the x-terms will be additive inverses.

$$\begin{aligned} 2(3x + 4y &= 2) \\ -3(2x + 6y &= -2) \end{aligned}$$

Then, add the two equations and solve for y.

$$\begin{aligned} 6x + 8y &= 4 \\ \underline{-6x - 18y} &\underline{= 6} \\ -10y &= 10 \\ y &= -1 \end{aligned}$$

Substitute –1 for y in either of the given equations and solve for x.

$$\begin{aligned} 3x + 4y &= 2 \\ 3x + 4(-1) &= 2 \\ 3x - 4 &= 2 \\ 3x &= 6 \\ x &= 2 \end{aligned}$$

The solution to the system of equations is $(2, -1)$.

9. D: Since $23 \times 4 = 92$ exactly, 92 is a multiple of 23. All other answers do not have 23 as a factor.

10. B: Since the events are mutually exclusive, the sum of their individual probabilities is 1.0. Subtracting 0.6 from 1.0 yields 0.4. Therefore, the correct choice is B.

11. B: The sequence $\frac{1}{5}\frac{1}{25}\frac{1}{125}\frac{1}{625}$ ... may be used to represent the situation. Substituting the initial value of $\frac{1}{5}$ and the common ratio of $\frac{1}{5}$ into the formula $S = \frac{a}{1-r}$:

$$S = \frac{\frac{1}{5}}{1-\frac{1}{5}} = \frac{\frac{1}{5}}{\frac{4}{5}} = \frac{1}{4}$$

12. B: Claus has \$20 to spend, so the amount he spends must be less than or equal to ($\leq$) \$20. The entrance fee of \$2.50 is only charged once, so it should not be multiplied by x. The cost of a ticket multiplied by x represents the cost of buying x tickets. The entrance fee plus the cost of the tickets is Claus's total cost: $2.50 + 2x \leq 20$.

13. B: The histogram only shows that there are eight trees between 70 and 75 feet tall. It does not show the individual heights of the trees. That information cannot be obtained from this graph.

14. A: The teacher is using a concrete representation of the concept in question, since the dice she is using are physical objects which help communicate the concept. Verbal, graphic, and pictorial are not correct since the student is not merely observing a discussion about the concept or looking at a graphic representation. Concrete representations often lead to more depth of knowledge and better retention of the concepts.

15. A: If $a < b$ and $a < c$, it does not necessary follow that $b < c$. For example, a could equal 3, b could equal 5, and c could equal 4.

16. D: This situation may be modeled by an arithmetic sequence, with a common difference of 4 and an initial value of 3. Substituting the common difference and initial value into the formula, $a_n = a_1 + (n-1)d$, gives $a_n = 3 + (n-1)(4)$, which simplifies to $a_n = 4n - 1$.

17. C: A number that is divisible by 6 is divisible by 2 and 3. A number is divisible by 2 if it is even, and it is divisible by 3 if the sum of the digits is divisible by 3. For example, the number 12 is divisible by 2 and 3, so it is also divisible by 6.

18. A: Marcus needs \$325 for the new gaming system. If he earns \$6.50 an hour, the number of hours he needs to work can be determined by dividing \$325 by \$6.50 which is written as $\frac{325}{6.50} = x$. Multiplying both sides of the equation by 6.50 yields $6.50x = 325$.

19. A: If $a|b$ and $a|c$, it does not necessarily follow that $b|c$. One counterexample is $3|6$ and $3|15$, but 6 does not divide 15.

20. B, D: The number 203.988 contains an 8 in the hundredths place and the thousandths place. Choices A and C are incorrect because they refer to the hundreds place and the thousands place. Choices B and D correctly describe the relationship between the hundredths and thousandths places. Hundredths are ten times larger than thousandths, and thousandths are ten times smaller than hundredths.

21. C: Since the linear equation is given in slope-intercept form ($y = mx + b$), start by identifying the y-intercept, which is represented by the variable b. The y-intercept is –3, so the graph of the line will intersect the y-axis at –3, or $(0, -3)$.

Next, identify the slope, which is represented by the variable m in the equation. The slope is 2, or $\frac{2}{1}$.

Recall that slope is rise over run. Starting from the y-intercept at point $(0, -3)$, move 2 units up and 1 unit to the right to find the next point on the graph. The coordinate pair for this point is $(1, -1)$. The graph that represents the linear equation $y = 2x - 3$ must include points $(0, -3)$ and $(1, -1)$. Since the graph shown in answer C contains both points, the correct answer is C.

22. D: We can use the table to find the linear equation in slope-intercept form, $y = mx + b$, where m is the slope and b is the y-intercept. The table shows the y-intercept (the y value at $x = 0$) to be -5. The slope is the ratio of the change in y-values to the corresponding change in x-values. As the x-value increases by 1, the y-value increases by 3. Thus, the slope is $\frac{3}{1}$, or 3. So the equation is $y = 3x - 5$.

Only the graphs in choices B and D have a y-intercept at -5. Of these two graphs, only choice D has a y-value increase of 3 for each x-value increase of 1, indicating a slope of 3.

23. C: Addition and subtraction of whole numbers up to 20 using concrete and pictorial models and number sentences is the appropriate level for first-grade students. Numbers up to 1,000 and number pairs are appropriate for third-grade students. Counting by ones and tens is appropriate for kindergarten.

24. A: If 18 of 24 students completed their projects, then 6 of 24 failed to do so. $\frac{6}{24} = \frac{1}{4}$.

25. B: The equation $y + 3 = 7$ is solved by subtracting 3 from both sides to yield $y = 4$. Substituting $y = 4$ into $x - 1 = y$ yields $x - 1 = 4$. Adding 1 to both sides of this equation yields $x = 5$.

26. D: The cross-section is a hexagon.

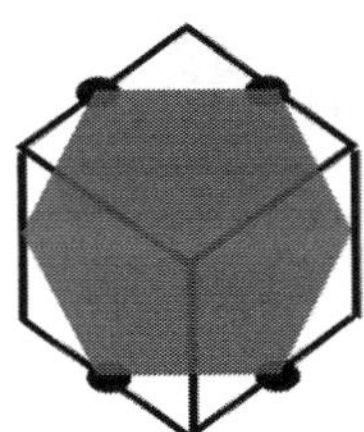

27. D: The perimeter of the triangle is equal to the sum of the side lengths. The length of the longer diagonal side may be represented as $d = \sqrt{(4-1)^2 + (5-2)^2}$, which simplifies to $d = \sqrt{18}$. The length of the shorter diagonal side may be represented as $d = \sqrt{(6-4)^2 + (2-5)^2}$, which simplifies to $d = \sqrt{13}$. The base length is 5 units. Thus, the perimeter is equal to $5 + \sqrt{18} + \sqrt{13}$, which is approximately 12.85 units. Since each unit represents 5 miles, the total distance she will have walked is equal to the product of 12.85 and 5, or approximately 64 miles.

28. C: Solving for x in an equation. Young children are not ready for algebraic equations, but they can learn to recognize patterns by counting by twos, comparing geometric shapes, and analyzing data they have collected.

29. A: A hexagon has six sides. A hexagonal prism has 8 faces consisting of two hexagonal bases and six rectangular lateral faces. This results in 18 edges and 12 vertices. Therefore, the correct choice is A.

30. D: The expression $(x-2)^2$ may be expanded as x^2-4x+4. Multiplication of $-3x$ by this expression gives $-3x^3+12x^2-12x$.

31. C: The probability of tossing a coin and getting heads is $\frac{1}{2}$. Multiply the probability by the number of coin tosses: $\frac{1}{2}\times 300=150$. You would expect to get heads about 150 times.

32. A: If Yu is paid every 2 weeks, the following proportion may be written: $\frac{60}{2}=\frac{x}{52}$. We cross-multiply to obtain the equation $2x=3{,}120$. Dividing both sides of the equation by 2 gives $x=1{,}560$.

33. A: First, state the exclusions of the domain.

$$\begin{gathered} x^3+3x^2-6x-8\neq 0 \\ (x-2)(x+4)(x+1)\neq 0 \\ x-2\neq 0 \quad x+4\neq 0 \quad x+1\neq 0 \\ x\neq 2 \qquad x\neq -4 \qquad x\neq -1 \end{gathered}$$

To determine whether there are asymptotes or holes at these values of x, simplify the expression:

$$\frac{x^2-2x-3}{x^3+3x^2-6x-8}=\frac{(x-3)(x+1)}{(x-2)(x+4)(x+1)}=\frac{x-3}{(x-2)(x+4)}$$

There are asymptotes at $x=2$ and at $x=-4$ and a hole at $x=-1$. Statement I is true.

To find the x-intercept of $f(x)$, solve $f(x)=0$. $f(x)=0$ when the numerator is equal to zero. The numerator equals zero when $x=3$ and $x=-1$; however, –1 is excluded from the domain of $f(x)$, so the x-intercept is 3. To find the y-intercept of $f(x)$, find $f(0)$.

$$\frac{0^2-2(0)-3}{0^3+3(0)^2-6(0)-8}=\frac{-3}{-8}=\frac{3}{8}$$

The x-intercept is 3, but the y-intercept is not 3. Statement II is false.

34. A: Since area is two dimensional, the units for area have an exponent of 2, such as in^2, yd^2, cm^2, or m^2. Choice B includes a unit of length (yd) and a unit of volume (yd^3). Choice C includes only units of length. Choice C includes a square unit of time (s^2). Therefore, the correct choice is A.

35. C: The expression representing the monthly charge for Company A is $\$25+\$0.05m$, where m is the time in minutes spent talking on the phone. Set this expression equal to the monthly charge for Company B, which is \$50. Solve for m to find the number of minutes the two companies charge the same amount.

$$\begin{aligned} \$25+\$0.05m &= \$50 \\ \$0.05m &= \$25 \\ m &= 500 \end{aligned}$$

Notice that the answer choices are given in hours, not in minutes. Since there are 60 minutes in an hour, $m=\frac{500}{60}$ hours $=8\frac{1}{3}$ hours. One-third of an hour is 20 minutes, so $m=8$ hours 20 minutes.

36. A: An operation is commutative if changing the order of the terms does not change the result. Addition and multiplication are commutative. Therefore, $8 + 12 = 12 + 8$ is an example of the commutative property.

37. B: The following proportion may be written and solved for x: $\frac{15 \text{ ft}}{5 \text{ ft}} = \frac{6 \text{ ft}}{x \text{ ft}}$. Cross multiplying results in $15x = 30$. Dividing by 15 gives $x = 2$. Thus, the shadow cast by the man is 2 feet in length.

38. C: The original price x may be modeled by the equation $(x - 0.35x) \times 1.0825 = 9.14$, which simplifies to $0.703625x = 9.14$. Dividing each side of the equation by the coefficient of x gives $x \approx 12.99$. The book was originally $12.99.

39. C: Remember the order of operations when solving this equation. First, simplify all operations inside parentheses. Second, simplify any exponential expressions. Third, perform all multiplications and divisions as they occur in the problem from left to right. Fourth, perform all additions and subtractions as they occur in the problem from left to right:

$$\begin{aligned} &2(7+8)^2 - 12(6 \times 2) \\ &= 2(15)^2 - 12(12) \\ &= 2(225) - 12(12) \\ &= 450 - 144 \\ &= 306 \end{aligned}$$

40. D: Since there are 100 homes' market times represented in each set, the median time a home spends on the market is between the 50th and 51st data point in each set. The 50th and 51st data points for Zip Code 1 are six months and seven months, respectively, so the median time a house in Zip Code 1 spends on the market is between six and seven months (6.5 months), which by the realtor's definition of market time is a seven-month market time. The 50th and 51st data points for Zip Code 2 are both thirteen months, so the median time a house in Zip Code 2 spends on the market is thirteen months. So, there is a six month difference between the median of Zip Code 1 and the median of Zip Code 2.

To find the mean market time for 100 houses, find the sum of the market times and divide by 100. If the frequency of a one-month market time is 9, the number 1 is added nine times (1×9), if frequency of a two-month market time is 10, the number 2 is added ten times (2×10), and so on. So, to find the average market time, divide by 100 the sum of the products of each market time and its corresponding frequency. For Zip Code 1, the mean market time is 7.38 months, which by the realtor's definition of market time is an eight-month market time. For Zip Code 2, the mean market time is 12.74, which by the realtor's definition of market time is a thirteen-month market time. So, the difference between the mean of Zip Code 1 and the mean of Zip Code 2 is 4 months.

The mode market time is the market time for which the frequency is the highest. For Zip Code 1, the mode market time is three months, and for Zip Code 2, the mode market time is eleven months. Therefore, the median time a house spends on the market in Zip Code 1 is less than the mean time a house spends on the market in Zip Code 1.

41. Scoring Rubric:

Constructed response items will be scored holistically on a scale of 1-4 according to the following performance indicators:

Completion	The degree to which the candidate addresses all parts of the prompt
Organization/Clarity	The degree to which the candidate presents their response and supporting evidence in an organized, coherent manner
Accuracy/Relevancy	The degree to which the candidate demonstrates meaningful and accurate knowledge and skills pertaining to the prompt
Use of supporting evidence	The degree to which the candidate uses specific, appropriate, and relevant examples and reasoning from the exhibits provided

Candidates that receive an overall score of "4" demonstrate excellent pedagogical knowledge and skills related to the prompt.

- All parts of the prompt are addressed with thoroughness and attention to detail
- Information in the response is very well-organized, clear, and accessible to the reader
- The response demonstrates accurate and relevant pedagogical knowledge and skills relative to all items in the prompt
- The response includes ample specific, appropriate, and relevant examples from the exhibits provided with detailed explanations

Arts and Sciences

1. B: Dimension, texture, and space are all *elements* of art, while unity is one of the *principles* of art. Unity in artwork is achieved when an artist's use of the elements produces a sense of wholeness or completeness in the finished product.

2. C: Paul Revere and William Dawes were both dispatch riders who set out on horseback from Massachusetts to spread news of British troop movements across the American countryside around the beginning of the War of Independence. John Parker was the captain of the Minutemen militia, who were waiting for the British at Lexington, Massachusetts. Samuel Prescott, a young physician, joined Paul Revere and William Dawes along their route.

3. D: In the Dred Scott decision of 1857, the Court ruled that no slave or descendant of slaves could ever be a United States citizen. It also declared the Missouri Compromise of 1820 to be unconstitutional, clearing the way for the expansion of slavery in new American territories. This ruling pleased Southerners and outraged the North, further dividing the nation and setting the stage for war.

4. D: Assigning students to write an essay comparing and contrasting the influence that two famous American artists or artworks had on US society would be most appropriate for helping high school students develop an appreciation for the value and role of art in US society. The other activities mentioned, including having students create a slide show presentation about a famous American artist, asking students to create a timeline showing when famous works of American art were created, and taking students on a field trip to an art museum, would not necessarily achieve this learning goal because they do not include it explicitly.

5. B: The Seven Years' War was a global military conflict. In the Americas, the conflict was largely between Western European countries, particularly Great Britain and France.

6. C: Physical geography focuses on processes and patterns in the natural environment. What people eat in any given geographic region is largely dependent on such environmental factors as climate and the availability of arable land. Religion, family, and language may all be affected by geographical factors, but they are not as immediately affected as dietary preferences.

7. B: An apple turning brown is an example of a chemical change; in this case, oxidation. During a chemical change, one substance is changed into another. Sublimation of water refers to the conversion between the solid and the gaseous phases of matter, with no intermediate liquid stage. This is a phase change, not a chemical reaction. Dissolution of salt in water refers to a physical change since the salt and water can be separated again by evaporating the water. Pulverized rock is an example of a physical change where the form has changed but not the substance itself.

8. B: It is true that rocks are classified by their formation and the minerals they contain, while minerals are classified by their chemical composition and physical properties. Choice A is incorrect because rocks may contain traces of organic compounds. Choices C and D are incorrect because only minerals can be polymorphs and only rocks contain mineraloids.

9. A: The eye wall of a hurricane has the strongest winds and the greatest rainfall. The eye wall is the tower-like rim of the eye. It is from this wall that clouds extend out, which are seen from above as the classic outward spiral pattern. A hurricane front is the outermost edge of its influence; although there will be heavy winds and rain in this area, the intensity will be relatively small. The eye of a hurricane is actually a place of surprising peace. In this area, dry and cool air rushes down to the ground or sea. Once there, the air is caught up in the winds of the eye wall and is driven outward at a furious pace.

10. D: Igneous rocks are formed when magma in the Earth erupts through cracks in the crust. There, the lava cools, creating a hard structure with many air pockets or holes.

11. D: The Bill of Rights was drafted by Congress to limit the authority of the government and protect the rights of individual citizens from abuse by the federal government. It was the first document to detail the rights of private citizens.

12. B: To develop perceptual-motor skills, it is best to engage students in physical activities that they find fun or enjoyable and that can be described and taught in terms of particular steps. These activities should involve uses of the senses such as sight, hearing, and touch. For example, shooting hoops can be described in particular steps. It involves holding the basketball, looking at the hoop, and shooting the basketball. If shooting hoops is an activity students enjoy, this is a good activity to help students develop perceptual-motor skills.

13. B: A fresco is actually a painting style that involves applying paint or pigment directly to plaster. In order to give pigment the desired consistency for fluid painting, several things can be mixed with the pigment: egg tempera; water; turpentine, which is used as a cleaner and thinner; or oil, which has the opposite effect to turpentine, making the paint thicker.

14. A: The 10th Amendment establishes that any power not given to the federal government in the Constitution belongs to the states or the people. The federal and local governments share many responsibilities.

15. A: The phenomenon of "sticky prices" refers to prices that stay the same even though it seems they should change (either increasing or decreasing).

16. A: The Age of Enlightenment was a time of scientific and philosophical achievement. Also called the Age of Reason, it was a time when human thought and reason were prized.

17. C: Thomas Jefferson embraced John Locke's concept of separation of church and state. Deism posits that a Supernatural force created the world and universe, but that He did not intervene after creation. Jefferson wanted minimal central governing, just as he viewed the Creator's relationship with the universe.

18. B: Gradualism states that evolution occurs slowly, with organisms exhibiting small changes over long periods of time. According to gradualism, the fossil record should show gradual changes over time. Punctuated equilibrium states that evolution occurs in spurts of sudden change. According to punctuated equilibrium, the fossil record should have large gaps.

19. C: There are no formal qualifications for members of the judicial branch. However, having a background in law is an informal qualification that is considered when appointing Article III judges.

20. C: Fossils are least likely to be found in igneous rock. Igneous rock is formed by extreme heat as magma escapes through the Earth's crust and cools. The remains of plants and animals in fossil form are not usually preserved under these conditions. Sedimentary rock (A) is where most fossils are found. Sedimentary rock is formed more slowly and is very abundant. Since soft mud and silts compress into layers, organisms can also be deposited. Metamorphic rock (B) is rock that has undergone change by heat and pressure. This usually destroys any fossils, but occasionally fossil remains are simply distorted and can be found in metamorphic rock.

21. B: The social interaction of students that aid or inhibit learning. According to these theories, students do not just learn in isolation or in a one-on-one relationship with a teacher. They also learn attitudes toward education from their peers, sometimes positive and sometimes negative.

22. B: Discretionary spending is dedicated to transportation, education, national resources, the environment, and international affairs. State and local governments use this money to help finance programs. Mandatory spending covers entitlements such as Medicare, Social Security, Federal Retirement, and Medicaid.

23. C: Allegro is a tempo that ranges between 120 and 168 beats per minute (bpm). While allegro can be thought of as a "quick" tempo, it is not as fast as presto, played between 168 and 200 bpm. Therefore, choice A is incorrect. Moderato and largo—played between 108-120 and 40-60, respectively—are slower tempos, proving choices B and D incorrect.

24. C: Vinegar fizzing when poured on a rock is an example of chemical weathering. Mechanical and chemical weathering are processes that break down rocks. Mechanical weathering breaks down rocks physically but does not change their chemical composition. Frost and abrasion are examples. Water, oxygen, carbon dioxide, and living organisms can lead to the chemical weathering of rock. Vinegar is a weak acid and will undergo a chemical reaction, evidenced by fizzing, with the rock. Choice A, rain freezing on the roadway, is an example of the phase change of water from a liquid to a solid and may lead to physical weathering. Choice B, ivy growing on the side of a wooden house, is incorrect since the house is not a rock. Choice D, a river carrying sediment downstream, is an example of erosion.

25. C: Covalent compounds are usually formed by the combination of two or more non-metallic elements with one another. In these compounds, atoms share electrons. Ionic compounds are most often formed between a metal and a nonmetal. Organic compounds are covalent compounds that contain carbon and hydrogen atoms. Some of the compounds formed by non-metallic elements are polar, but not all of them.

26. C: The Mason-Dixon Line was the manifestation of a border dispute between the British colonies of Pennsylvania, Maryland, and Delaware. It effectively separated, or illustrated, a cultural divide between North and South before the Civil War.

27. D: Chemical equations must be balanced on each side of the reaction. Balancing means the total number of atoms stays the same, but their arrangement within specific reactants and products can change. The law of conservation of matter states that matter can never be created or destroyed. Heat may be absorbed or released in a reaction; these are classified as endothermic and exothermic reactions, respectively. The rate of the reaction increases with temperature for most reactions.

28. D: The equation for power, $power = \frac{work}{time}$, can be utilized. The mass of the object (10 kg) and the distance (10 m) can be used to calculate work, $work = mass \times (gravitational\ acceleration) \times distance$. The value for time is provided.

29. A: Before drawing a conclusion about a hypothesis, one should test it, observe it, and record data about the test results. In the discussion of many scientific papers, scientists will compare and contrast their data to the findings of other groups. The methods of an experiment should be written so an experiment can be replicated.

30. D: The temperature of a substance during the time of any phase change remains the same. In this case, the phase change was from liquid to solid, or freezing. Latent heat of fusion, in this case, is energy that is released from the substance as it reforms its solid form. This energy will be released and the liquid will turn to solid before the temperature of the substance will decrease further. If the substance were changing from solid to liquid, the heat of fusion would be the amount of heat required to break apart the attractions between the molecules in the solid form to change to the liquid form. The latent heat of fusion is exactly the same quantity of energy for a substance for either melting or freezing. Depending on the process, this amount of heat would either be absorbed by the substance (melting) or released (freezing).

31. A: Checks and balances were established to keep one branch of government from taking too much authority. When Johnson violated the Tenure of Office Act by replacing Secretary of War Edwin Stanton, Johnson was impeached, but the final vote in the Senate trial came up one vote short of the number needed to convict him.

32. A: Animals of the phylum Mollusca respire through gills. Respiration is the process of taking in oxygen and releasing carbon dioxide. Mollusks include five classes that include species as diverse as chitons, land and marine snails, and squid. This represents a diverse range of body structures. Many mollusks have a mantle that includes a cavity that is used for both breathing and excretion. Within the mantle are gills (ctenidia). Mollusks do not have tracheas. Some land snails have reduced gills that feature a respiratory cavity but are not true lungs. Muscle contraction is not required for ventilation of the gills. Other structures, such as cilia, work to pass water over the gills.

33. C: Lying at a little more than 23° south of the equator, the Tropic of Capricorn is the border between the Southern Temperate Zone to the south and the Tropical Zone to the north. The southern hemisphere is tilted toward the sun to its maximum extent each year at the winter solstice in December. The northernmost latitude at which the sun can appear directly overhead is at the Tropic of Cancer during the summer solstice. The northern and southern hemispheres are separated by the equator at 0° latitude. The eastern and western hemispheres are separated by the prime meridian at 0° longitude.

34. A: Descriptive studies look at and analyze the characteristics of a population or compare aspects across multiple populations. These studies seek information about the state of a population as it is rather than experimentally investigating cause-and-effect relationships by manipulating variables and observing outcomes. Comparing the heights of male and female penguins is an example of a descriptive study. The subject is strictly an observable measure (height) of established populations (male and female). For the other studies, the focus is on the cause-and-effect relationship between a manipulated variable (different media, drug vs. placebo, and old vs. new descriptions) and a result of interest (growth rate, drug efficacy, sales).

35. A: The inaccurate statement is the Puritans unconditionally supported the English Reformation. While they agreed with the Reformation in principle, they felt that it had not pursued those principles far enough and should make greater reforms. Similarly, they felt that the Church of England (or Anglican Church), though it had separated from the Catholic Church in the Protestant Reformation, still allowed many practices they found too much like Catholicism. The Puritans did become a chief political power in England because of the first English Civil War between Royalists and Parliamentarians. The Royalists had a profound suspicion of the radical Puritans. Among the Parliament's elements of resistance, the strongest was that of the Puritans. They joined in the battle initially for ostensibly political reasons as others had, but soon they brought more attention to religious issues. Following the Restoration in 1660 and the Uniformity Act of 1662, thereby restoring the Church of England to its pre-English Civil War status, the great majority of Puritan clergy defected from the Church of England. It is also accurate that the Puritans in England disagreed about separating from the Church of England. Some Puritans desired complete separation; they were known first as Separatists and after the Restoration as Dissenters. Others did not want complete separation but instead desired further reform in the Church of England. While they remained part of the Church of England, they were called Non-Separating Puritans, and after the Restoration, they were called Nonconformists.

36. B: Temperature is a measure of the kinetic energy of particles. As temperature increases, the average kinetic energy also increases. As the gas particles move more rapidly, they occupy a larger volume. The increase in speed of the individual particles combined with the greater distance over which any intermolecular forces must act results in a decrease in the intermolecular forces.

37. A: Choice A is correct because second grade students should be able to calculate how money saved can accumulate into a larger amount over time. Choice D, which is expected of first grade students, is too basic for second grade. Choice C is expected of third grade students. Choice B is expected of fifth grade students. Therefore, the correct choice is A.

38. D: Johannes Brahms composed music in the middle to late 19th century. Therefore, Brahms is most strongly associated with the Romantic Period in classical music, which ran from about 1815 to about 1910. Bach is most strongly associated with the Baroque Period (1600-1760), and Ravel is most closely associated with the Impressionist Period (1890-1940). Aaron Copland, often is considered "the dean of American composers" and composed music in the mid to late 20th century; he would not fit into any of the above listed periods.

39. A: Rivers promoted the development of the ancient river valley civilizations of the world, including in the Middle East, India, and China. Rivers not only supply water for drinking and crop irrigation, but also provide fertile soil, vegetation for shade cover, food, building materials, and animal life. They additionally allow water travel to other locations. Although some peoples have settled and lived in deserts, they are among the most inhospitable climates. Forests also provide plenty of flora and fauna and exist in areas receiving enough rainfall, but rivers have been historically superior in attracting human societies. Mountains near living areas provide protective barriers; however, though some peoples live there, as in deserts, living in the mountains is difficult due to high altitudes, harsh climates, poor soil for planting, and rough terrain.

40. A: In the food chain of tree → caterpillar → frog → snake → hawk → worm, the tree is at the trophic level with the greatest amount of energy. Trophic level refers to the position of an organism in a food chain. Energy is lost according to the laws of thermodynamics as one moves up the food chain because it is converted to heat when consumers consume. Primary producers, such as autotrophs, are organisms who are at the base and capture solar energy. Primary consumers are herbivores that feed on the producers. Secondary consumers consume primary consumers and so on. Decomposers get their energy from the consumption of dead plants and animals.

Practice Test #2

Literacy and English Language Arts

1. A student is taking a reading test. The teacher has blocked out a number of words. Each blank is assigned a set of three possible words. The student must select the correct word from each set so that the text makes sense. The student is taking:

a. A cloze test
b. A daze test
c. A multiple-choice quiz
d. A vocabulary test

2. Which of the following reflects MLA guidelines for citing internet sources with regard to page numbers in in-text citations in research papers?

a. A source from the internet should not be used if it does not include page numbers in any form.
b. If a printout from a website has page numbers, citations should include these numbers.
c. In-text citations of online sources in research papers should never include page numbers.
d. If the source is a PDF file, the page numbers from the file should be in citations.

3. Among assessments of reading comprehension, which of these compares student scores to the average scores of a sample of students representing the same population?

a. A norm-referenced state test
b. An informal reading inventory
c. A curriculum-based assessment
d. A criterion-referenced state test

4. Context clues are useful in:

a. Predicting future action
b. Understanding the meaning of words that are not familiar
c. Understanding character motivation
d. Reflecting on a text's theme

5. A teacher designs lessons for the upcoming week. During the first part of the week, the teacher is going to divide the class into two sections. While one group is working independently on their projects, the other group will sit in a circle. The teacher has broken a story up into several sections, and each student will read a section aloud. The teacher will note for her records how many errors a student makes. She will also administer a brief verbal "quiz" to which the students will respond in writing. The combination of verbal reading results and comprehension quiz results will give her a better understanding of each child's abilities and/or needs. What kind of assessment did this teacher use?

a. Cloze-style
b. Informal reading inventory
c. Student response form
d. Articulation assessment

6. Phonemic awareness is a type of:

a. Phonological awareness. Phonemic awareness is the ability to recognize sounds within words.
b. Phonics. It is a teaching technique whereby readers learn the relationship between letters and sounds.
c. Alphabetization. Unless a reader knows the alphabet, phonemic awareness is useless.
d. Syntactical awareness. Understanding the underlying structure of a sentence is key to understanding meaning.

7. Which of the following statements is correct regarding Standard English?

a. Standard English does not include dialects.
b. Rules from Standard English apply to written language.
c. Standard English is universal in English-speaking nations.
d. No Standard English exists that is actually used in practice.

8. A teacher has given her students an assignment to write a non-rhyming poem of three lines. The first and last lines each contain five syllables, and the middle line contains seven syllables. The students are writing a:

a. Limerick
b. Metaphor
c. Villanelle
d. Haiku

9. A class is about to read a science book about fossils. Before they begin, she writes the words *stromatolites, fossiliferous,* and *Eocene* on the board. She explains the meaning of each word. These words are examples of:

a. Academic words
b. Alliteration
c. Content-specific words
d. Ionization

10. Which choice most appropriately fills the blanks in this statement? "In writing, _____ is the writer's attitude as evident from the writing, and _____ is the individual way in which the writer expresses themselves through the writing."

a. voice, tone
b. tone, voice
c. style, tone
d. voice, style

11. A teacher asks her students to say the word *map*. She then says, "Change the /m/ sound to a /t/ sound. What word do you have now?" Which phonemic awareness skill are students practicing?

a. Alliteration
b. Segmenting
c. Blending onset and rime
d. Phoneme substitution

12. The English language word *noob* is an example of the result of which linguistic process?

a. Blending
b. Conversion
c. Neologisms
d. Onomatopoeia

13. Another name for a persuasive essay is:

a. Dynamic essay
b. Convincing essay
c. Argumentative essay
d. Position paper

14. Which choice describes the most complete method of displaying student achievement or progress in language arts?

a. A written report or story that demonstrates a student's knowledge of grammar, spelling, comprehension, and writing skills.
b. Either a norm- or criterion-referenced test that breaks language skills into small subsets and provides achievement levels for each skill.
c. A portfolio containing a log of stories or books the student has read, rates of reading fluency, writing samples, creative projects, and spelling, grammar, and comprehension tests/quizzes.
d. A year-end project in which the student presents what he or she has learned from a student-chosen book; the student must read an excerpt of the story and display a visual aid highlighting important information from the story or literary techniques used by the author.

15. A teacher writes four sentences on the board and instructs his students to copy the sentences from the board into their notebooks. They must capitalize words with suffixes. Which sentence is correct?

a. The PRINCE declared his undying love for the PRINCESS.
b. Television is a form of MULTIMEDIA.
c. This loud, loud noise is very DISPLEASING.
d. The BOOKKEEPER examined every page of the rare play.

16. *Train, brain, spring.* The underlined letters are examples of:

a. Consonant digraph
b. Consonant blend
c. Consonant shift
d. Continental shift

17. Which of the following is the correct sequence of these phases of spelling development?

a. Semiphonetic, precommunicative, transitional, correct, phonetic
b. Precommunicative, semiphonetic, phonetic, transitional, correct
c. Correct, phonetic, semiphonetic, precommunicative, transitional
d. Phonetic, semiphonetic, transitional, correct, precommunicative

18. A reading teacher is assessing an eighth grader to determine her reading level. Timed at a minute, the student reads with 93% accuracy. She misreads an average of seven words out of 100. What is her reading level?

a. She is reading at a Frustration level.
b. She is reading at an Excellence level.
c. She is reading at an Instructional level.
d. She is reading at an Independent level.

19. "Decoding" is also called:

a. Remediation
b. Deciphering
c. Alphabetic principle
d. Deconstruction

20. Which of the following would be most useful in assessing and documenting students' language progress throughout a school year?

a. An audio/video recording of each student reading the same text at the beginning of the year and again at the end of the year
b. A portfolio including pre-tests, post-tests, vocabulary work, journal entries, writing assignments, group projects, and other relevant work from throughout the year
c. Score composites and details from state- and national-referenced exams or other standardized tests.
d. A detailed narrative composed by the student's teacher, detailing strengths, weaknesses, and descriptions of the student's work.

21. Following a typical developmental sequence, which of the following is expected of second graders in decoding and identifying new or unfamiliar words?

a. Identifying new words and compound words via phonics, roots, suffixes, and analogies
b. Identifying new word meanings through knowledge of familiar synonyms and antonyms
c. Identifying new word meanings by comparing to known homophones and homographs
d. Identifying new word meanings by roots, prefixes, suffixes, idioms, and dictionary markings

22. The teacher and her students brainstorm a list of talents, skills, and specialized knowledge belonging to members of the class. Some of the items on the list include how to make a soufflé, how to juggle, and how to teach a dog to do tricks. One student knows a great deal about spiders, and another knows about motorcycles. The teacher asks the students to each write an essay about something they are good at or know a great deal about. What kind of essay is she asking the students to produce?

a. Cause and effect
b. Compare/contrast
c. Expository
d. Argumentative

23. Word-recognition ability is:

a. Equally important to all readers
b. Used only by fluent readers
c. Another term for "word attack"
d. Especially important to English language learners and students with reading disabilities

24. Ms. Baird wants to check her students' individual comprehension skills, specifically their ability to support an idea with evidence from a text. Which scenario is the best way to accomplish her goals?

a. Split the students into groups after reading the text as a class and allow them to work together on a worksheet activity she has designed.
b. Play a game in which Ms. Baird posts a card with a main idea. Students read silently and independently and raise their hands to answer when they have found a transition in the plot.
c. As a class, brainstorm main ideas, topics, or concepts from a text. Allow students to choose a select number of these ideas and copy them onto separate index cards. The students then should individually review the text, recording any supporting evidence on the notecard with the applicable main idea.
d. Administer a comprehension quiz during class. Allow students to switch papers and grade each other's work. Next, students can spend the remainder of the class period discussing the answers so that each one understands the text fully.

25. Syllable types include:

a. Closed, open, silent *e*, vowel team, vowel-*r*, and consonant-*le*
b. Closed, open, silent, double-vowel, *r*, and *le*
c. Closed, midway, open, emphasized, prefixed, and suffixed
d. Stressed, unstressed, and silent

26. Examples of CVC words include:

a. Add, pad, mad
b. Cat, tack, act
c. Elephant, piano, examine
d. Dog, sit, leg

27. The phrase "pretty as a picture" is best described as a:

a. Metaphor
b. Simile
c. Duodenum's couple
d. Figure of speech

28. *Since, whether,* and *accordingly* are examples of which type of signal words?

a. Common, or basic, signal words
b. Compare/contrast words
c. Cause–effect words
d. Temporal sequencing words

29. According to the MLA guidelines for in-text citations in research papers, when can the citation include one author's name and *et al* for any other authors of a single source?

a. When there is more than one author
b. When there are two or three authors
c. When there are three or more authors
d. When there are four or more authors

30. A classroom is comprised of students with varying abilities in language. Some students can read fluently, while others are still just learning. Speech and language abilities also range widely among the students. Which approach best suits this class?

a. Each student begins with reading texts slightly below their ability level and practices reading aloud with partners and teachers to build skills.
b. The teacher consistently presents challenging material for students, knowing that when students are held to high expectations, they typically rise to meet a challenge.
c. The teacher splits the classroom into groups based on ability and appoints a group leader to guide other students.
d. The class is exposed to a variety of "texts," in combination with direct phonetic and vocabulary instruction, including written text, video, song, and spoken stories.

31. A teacher is working with a group of English language learners. She asks them to take two pieces of paper. At the top of the first paper, they are to write *SAME*, and at the top of the other, *DIFFERENT*. Each child will consider what his native country and the United States have in common, and what distinct features each country possesses. The children are using which method in organizing their ideas?

a. Hunt and peck
b. Consider and persuade
c. Evaluate and contrast
d. Compare and contrast

32. Which of the following statements regarding the acquisition of language is false?

a. Young children often have the ability to comprehend written language just as early as they can comprehend or reproduce oral language when given appropriate instruction.
b. Oral language typically develops before a child understands the relationship between spoken and written words.
c. Most young children are first exposed to written language when an adult reads aloud.
d. A child's ability to speak, read, and write depends on a variety of physiological factors, as well as environmental factors.

33. Of the following statements, which is true about the relationship of reading fluency, word decoding, and reading comprehension?

a. Developing fluency in reading has no relationship to speed and automaticity with decoding words.
b. Students should have strong word recognition foundations established before fluency instruction.
c. Reading fluency shows faster information processing speed, but has no impact on comprehension.
d. Slower, less automatic word decoding decreases reading fluency, but it increases comprehension.

34. Which of the following statements is most true?

a. Introducing oral and written texts from a variety of cultures can enhance students' understanding and appreciation of language.
b. Children typically learn language best when exposed primarily to texts exemplary of their own background or culture, thereby increasing their ability to identify personally with what they are learning.
c. Studying other languages will impair a student's ability to develop his or her own first language.
d. Students should be exposed to one type of text at a time to diminish genre confusion.

35. A writing assignment asks the student to do things like organize, plan, formulate, assemble, compose, construct, or arrange some material they have read or learned. Which of the following cognitive (learning) objectives is the teacher aiming to meet with this assignment?

a. Analysis
b. Synthesis
c. Evaluation
d. Application

36. What is the purpose of targeted instruction?

a. Deliver instructions that are precise, clear, and direct so that students understand exactly what is expected.
b. Accurately rank a group of learners from low achievers to high achievers so that the teacher knows from the beginning of the school year which students have less ability and will therefore need support.
c. Teach students how to take information from a text and reorganize it into bulleted lists.
d. Assess and target areas needing improvement as well as areas of greatest strength for each student to ensure that all members of a class are receiving instruction tailored to their specific needs.

37. Which choice describes a primary benefit of an adult reading aloud to a group of elementary students?

a. Students have a chance to rest their minds and enjoy oral language.
b. The adult can model reading fluently for students still building reading skills.
c. Students have time and opportunity to work on individual projects and assignments while listening to the story.
d. The adult transmits a great deal of conceptual knowledge via auditory instruction, which is especially beneficial for students who are auditory learners.

38. What is a mnemonic device?

a. A saying or image used to help remember a complex concept
b. A tool that increases physical relaxation during a test
c. An old-fashioned torture device involving repeated testing
d. A tool for selecting answers on tests

39. An eighth-grade student is able to decode most words fluently and has a borderline/acceptable vocabulary, but his reading comprehension is quite low. He can be helped with instructional focus on:

a. Strategies to increase comprehension and to build vocabulary
b. Strategies to increase comprehension and to be able to identify correct syntactical usage
c. Strategies to improve his understanding of both content and context
d. Strategies to build vocabulary and to improve his understanding of both content and context

40. Which of the following statements is most accurate about writing the introduction of an essay?

a. The introduction should move from the broad and general to the focused and specific.
b. The introduction should save the most attention-getting material for later in the work.
c. The introduction should move from the focused and specific to the broad and general.
d. The introduction should use the technique of starting essays with dictionary definitions.

41. 400-600 word response

In this constructed response activity, you will be presented with a sample of a student's response to an assignment. You must respond by identifying a student's noteworthy strengths and their weaknesses, presenting evidence of each. Then, you must describe how you would provide an instructional intervention which builds from the student's strength to address the student's needs. Then explain how your intervention will be effective in meeting the student's needs. Your response should be between 400 and 600 words.

Exhibit 1: Lesson goal

Mrs. Harris, a 2nd-grade teacher is assessing Charlie's reading comprehension of a story that he reads fluently and accurately by having Charlie retell the story in his own words. The goal of this activity is to assess and improve on reading comprehension and paraphrasing ability.

Exhibit 2: Reading material

Bobby is at the park. He plays a new game. A boy tells him how to play the game. First, Bobby has to run as fast as he can. He likes to run. When he runs fast, he feels like he is flying.

Next, the boy says, "Red light!" Bobby has to stop. He must stand very still. Then the boy says, "Green light!" Now, Bobby can run again. He runs fast. Bobby likes the new game. He wants to play it with his friend Jimmy at school.

Exhibit 3: Conversation transcript

Teacher: Can you tell me what you were reading about?

Charlie: It's a story about some boys. One boy is named Bobby. He doesn't know how to cross the street.

Teacher: How do you know that Bobby needs to learn about crossing the street?

Charlie: Because he doesn't even know about red lights and green lights. How red is for stop and green is for go. I think he's a little kid.

Teacher: What happens to Bobby in this story?

Charlie: This other boy bosses him around. Bobby wants to pretend he is flying. The other boy makes him stop. He yells, "Red light!" and then Bobby stops. I think the other boy tells him about the street when the cars stop. So, he learns about it.

Teacher: What else do you think Bobby will do?

Charlie: Maybe he'll tell the boy to stop bossing him around.

Response

Provide a response between 400 and 600 words on a separate piece of paper.

Mathematics

1. Which of the following options represents equivalency between mathematical expressions?

a. $3 + x + 3x + 3 + x = 5x + 6$
b. $7x - 2x = 9x$
c. $2y + 2y + 2y = 6y^3$
d. $2.5(x + 2) = 2.5x + 2$

2. Which of the following is the graph of the equation $y = -4x - 6$?

a.

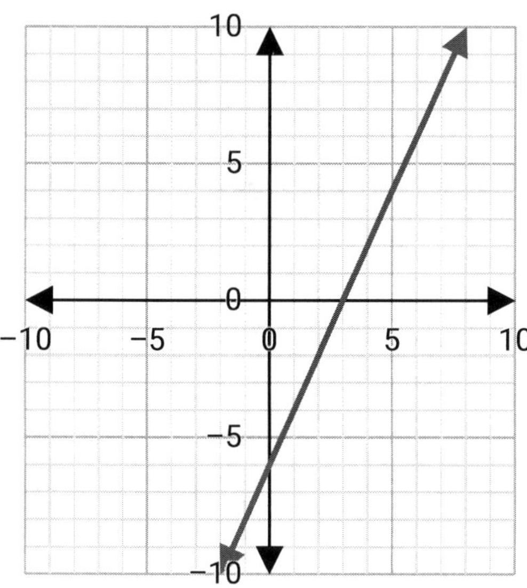

b.

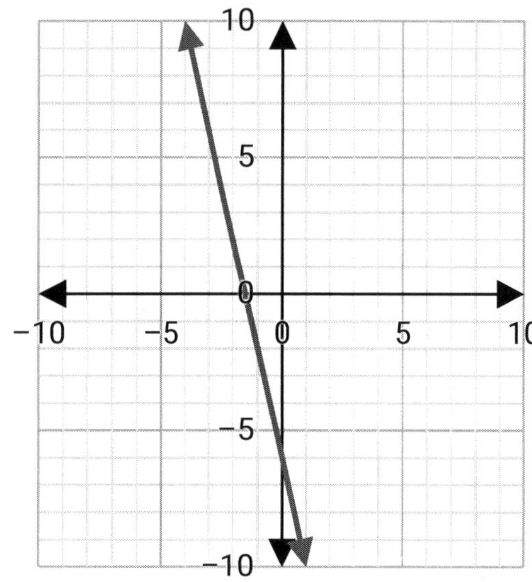

c.

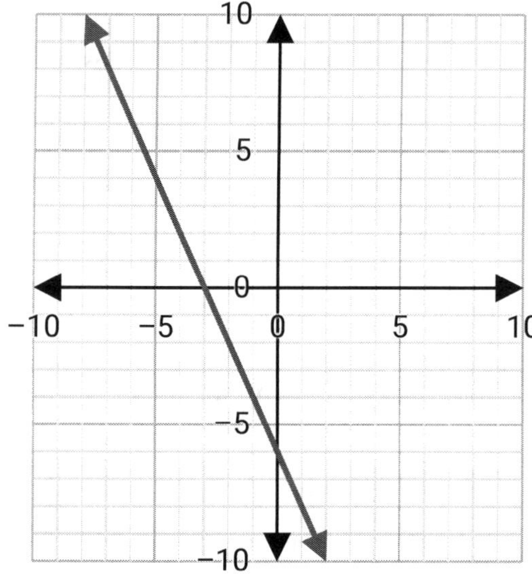

d.

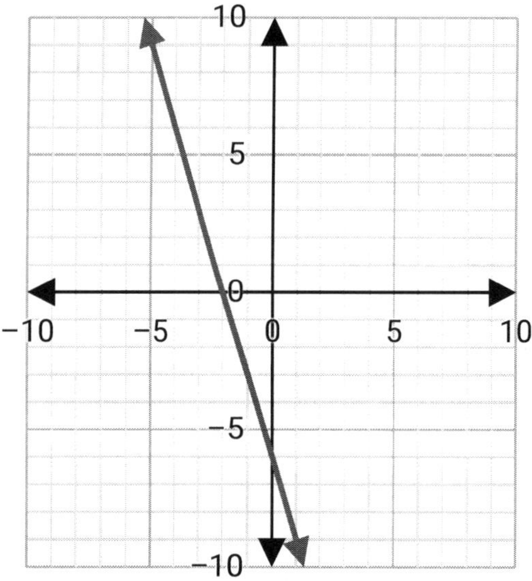

3. Which of these would best illustrate change over time?

a. Pie chart
b. Line graph
c. Box-and-whisker plot
d. Venn diagram

4. $f(x) = \frac{2-x}{4x}$**. What is the equation of the horizontal asymptote?**

a. $y = -\frac{1}{4}$
b. $y = -\frac{1}{2}$
c. $y = -2$
d. $y = 2$

5. Mr. Sarver, a second-grade teacher, notices that a few of his students are struggling with the concept of borrowing when subtracting two-digit numbers. Which of the following activities would best help students understand this concept of borrowing?

a. The teacher works subtraction problems on the whiteboard.
b. The students watch a children's video about borrowing.
c. The students complete a worksheet with subtraction problems.
d. The students use cardboard manipulatives to model subtraction problems.

6. A missing object problem like the one below is one way of helping students learn what concept?

Truck car bike train truck car bike ______ truck car bike train

a. Counting
b. Problem solving
c. Manipulation of objects
d. Basic addition

7. The scientific notation for a particular amount is 1.62×10^{-2}**. What is this amount in standard form?**

a. 162
b. 1.62
c. 0.0162
d. 0.000162

8. What is most appropriate for young children to learn and practice measurement as an early mathematical skill?

a. Adults should discourage children's choosing measuring units and teach standard ones immediately.
b. Letting young children choose their own measurement units (like toys) promotes early development.
c. When children help with everyday activities, discussing measurement will make participation less fun.
d. Adults can let children express measurements using toys, etc., but should not also do this themselves.

9. Which expression is represented by the diagram below?

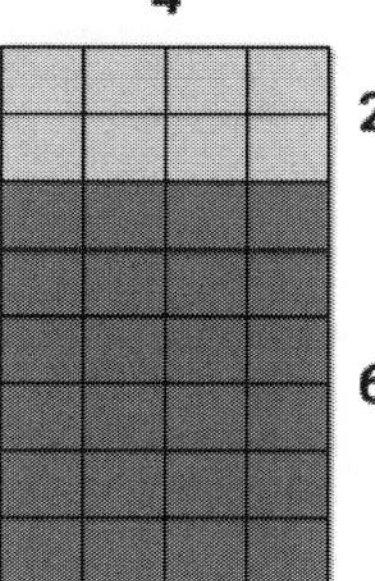

a. $4 \times (2 + 6)$
b. $4 \times (2 \times 6)$
c. $4 + (2 \times 6)$
d. $4 + (2 + 6)$

Refer to the following for question 10:

The box-and-whisker plot displays student test scores by class period.

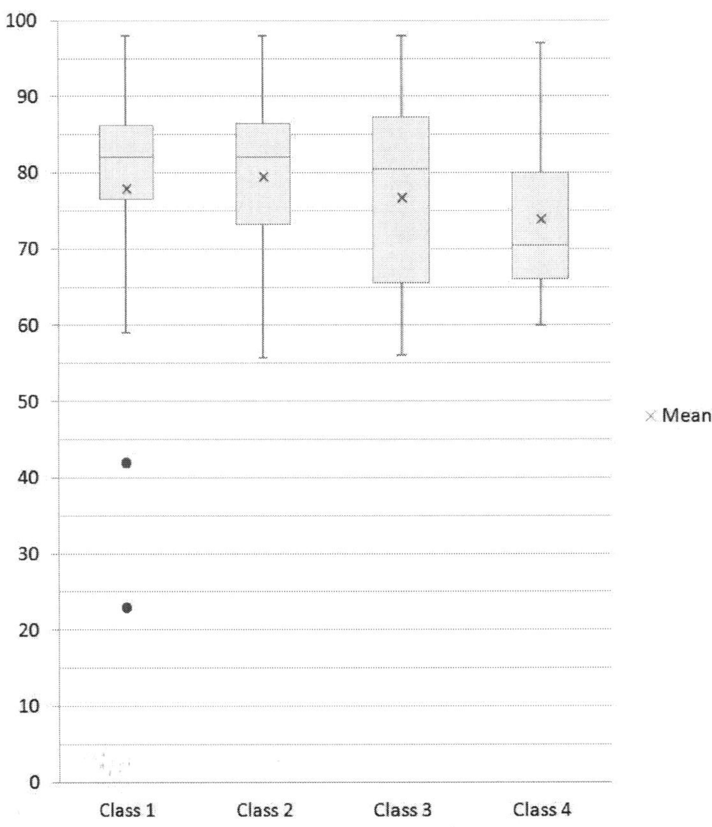

10. Which of the following statements is true of the data?

a. The mean better reflects student performance in class 1 than the median.
b. The mean test score for class 1 and 2 is the same.
c. The median test score for class 1 and 2 is the same.
d. The median test score is above the mean for class 4.

11. A student is asked to find the factors of 32. She comes up with the following list: 1, 2, 4, 8, 16, 32. Is this list correct?

a. Yes, it includes all the factors of 32.
b. Yes, but it omits several additional possible factors.
c. No, it contains several terms that are not factors of 32.
d. No, it is a list of the multiples rather than the factors of 32.

12. Kim's current monthly rent is $800. She is moving to another apartment complex, where the monthly rent will be $1,100. What is the percent increase in her monthly rent amount?

a. 25.5%
b. 27%
c. 35%
d. 37.5%

13. Mountain View Middle School is hosting the State Track and Field Meet. The girls' 200-meter race was an extremely tight race. The fastest time wins the race. The time for each racer is listed below.

Erin: 26.58 seconds
Baily: 26.06 seconds
Maria: 26.85 seconds
Larkin: 26.68 seconds
June: 28.05 seconds

Based on the race times, which statements are true? Select all that apply.

a. Baily won 1st place and June came in 2nd place.
b. June came in 5th place.
c. Baily, Erin, and Larkin were the fastest three runners.
d. Larkin ran the race one tenth of a second slower than Erin.

14. What is the educational purpose of having students measure the length of an object, such as their desk or table, with non-standard measuring units smaller than the object, such as crayons?

a. Measuring with small units is easier for young children
b. Children cannot read the markings on a standard ruler or yard stick
c. Students learn to measure something larger than a unit with repetitive use of that unit
d. Students will later be able to transfer measurements from meters to yards

15. Zeke drove from his house to a furniture store in Atlanta and then back home along the same route. It took Zeke three hours to drive to the store. By driving an average of 20 mph faster on his return trip, Zeke was able to save an hour of driving time. What was Zeke's average driving speed on his round trip?

a. 24 mph
b. 48 mph
c. 50 mph
d. 60 mph

16. A dartboard consists of two concentric circles with radii of 3 inches and 6 inches. If a dart is thrown onto the board, what is the probability the dart will land in the inner circle?

a. $\frac{1}{4}$
b. $\frac{1}{2}$
c. $\frac{1}{3}$
d. $\frac{1}{5}$

17. What is the constant of proportionality represented by the table below?

x	y
2	−8
5	−20
7	−28
10	−40
11	−44

a. −12
b. −8
c. −6
d. −4

18. A ball has a diameter of 7 inches. Which of the following best represents the volume?

a. 165.7 in^3
b. 179.6 in^3
c. 184.5 in^3
d. 192.3 in^3

19. Which of the following statements is true?

a. The set of whole numbers is a subset of the set of rational numbers.
b. The set of integers is a subset of the set of whole numbers.
c. The set of rational numbers is a subset of the set of whole numbers.
d. The set of whole numbers is a subset of the set of natural numbers.

20. Andrea must administer $\frac{1}{12}$ of a medicine bottle to a patient. If the bottle contains $3\frac{4}{10}$ fluid ounces of medicine, how much medicine should be administered?

a. $\frac{17}{60}$ fluid ounces
b. $\frac{15}{62}$ fluid ounces
c. $\frac{3}{19}$ fluid ounces
d. $\frac{17}{67}$ fluid ounces

21. What is the distance on a coordinate plane from $(-8, 6)$ to $(4, 3)$?

a. $\sqrt{139}$
b. $\sqrt{147}$
c. $\sqrt{153}$
d. $\sqrt{161}$

22. The expression $(2x + 3)(x - 2)$ can also be written as $2x^2 - x - 6$. Which of the following choices makes this transformation possible?

a. The distributive property
b. The commutative property
c. The associative property
d. The transformative property

23. Marlon pays $45 for a jacket that has been marked down 25%. What was the original cost of the jacket?

a. $80
b. $75
c. $65
d. $60

24. Coach Weybright's 6th-grade basketball team has played 36 games this season. The ratio of wins to losses is 2 : 1. If x represents the number of wins, which of the following proportions can be used to determine the number of wins?

a. $\frac{x}{36} = \frac{2}{1}$
b. $\frac{x}{2} = \frac{1}{36}$
c. $\frac{x}{3} = \frac{36}{2}$
d. $\frac{x}{36} = \frac{2}{3}$

25. For which of these does a rotation of 120° about the center of the polygon map the polygon onto itself?

a. Square
b. Regular hexagon
c. Regular octagon
d. Regular decagon

26. A developer decides to build a fence around a neighborhood park, which is positioned on a rectangular lot. Rather than fencing along the lot line, he fences x feet from each of the lot's boundaries. By fencing a rectangular space 141 yd^2 smaller than the lot, the developer saves $432 in fencing materials, which cost $12 per linear foot. How much does he spend?

a. $160
b. $456
c. $3,168
d. The answer cannot be determined from the given information.

27. A gift box has a length of 14 inches, a height of 8 inches, and a width of 6 inches. How many square inches of wrapping paper are needed to wrap the box?

a. 56
b. 244
c. 488
d. 672

28. Which of the following options represents equivalency between different representations of rational numbers?

a. $16 \div (6 - 4)^2 = 64$
b. $8 - 2(7 - 4) = 18$
c. $2^3 \div 2 - 2(2) = 0$
d. $2 + 3(2^2) = 20$

29. Which of the following equations may be used to convert $0.\overline{7}$ to a fraction?

a. $9x = 7.\overline{7} - 0.\overline{7}$
b. $99x = 7.\overline{7} - 0.\overline{7}$
c. $9x = 77.\overline{7} - 7.\overline{7}$
d. $90x = 7.\overline{7} - 0.\overline{7}$

30. Which of the following pairs of equations represents the lines of symmetry in the figure below?

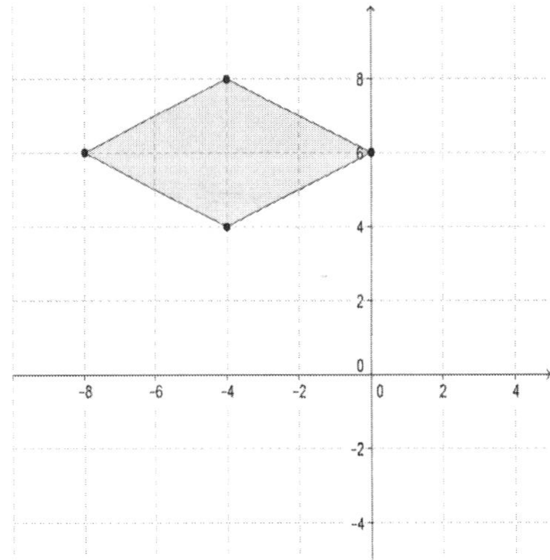

a. $x = -4, y = 6$
b. $x = 4, y = 6$
c. $y = -4, x = 6$
d. $y = 4, x = -6$

31. Addison tosses a six-sided die twelve times and records the results in the table below.

Toss	1	2	3	4	5	6	7	8	9	10	11	12
Results	2	5	1	2	3	6	6	2	4	5	4	3

Which of the following statements is true?

a. The experimental probability of tossing a 6 is greater than the theoretical probability.
b. The experimental probability of tossing a 3 is greater than the theoretical probability.
c. The experimental probability of tossing a 1 is greater than the theoretical probability.
d. The experimental probability of tossing a 2 is greater than the theoretical probability.

32. Eli rolls a six-sided die and tosses a coin. What is the probability that he gets a prime number or tails?

a. $\frac{1}{4}$
b. $\frac{1}{3}$
c. $\frac{1}{2}$
d. $\frac{3}{4}$

33. Which of the following statements is true?

a. A number is divisible by 3 if the sum of the digits is divisible by 3.
b. A number is divisible by 4 if the last digit is divisible by 2.
c. A number is divisible by 7 if the sum of the digits is divisible by 7.
d. A number is divisible by 6 if the sum of the last two digits is divisible by 6.

34. Which number comes next in the sequence?

16, 24, 34, 46, 60

a. 56
b. 72
c. 74
d. 76

35. During an activity, Mrs. Schwartz instructs her students to place coins into three groups, where each group gets progressively lower in total value. Which of the following students correctly completed this activity?

a. Henry with Group 1: 2 dimes, 2 nickels, and 4 pennies; Group 2: 1 dime, 3 nickels, 2 pennies; Group 3: 2 dimes, 1 nickel, 4 pennies
b. Graham with Group 1: 1 dime, 5 nickels, and 5 pennies; Group 2: 2 dimes, 2 nickels, 8 pennies; Group 3: 1 dime, 2 nickel, 9 pennies
c. Landon with Group 1: 3 dimes, 4 nickels, and 9 pennies; Group 2: 2 dimes, 4 nickels, 3 pennies; Group 3: 1 dime, 9 nickels, 2 pennies
d. Elizabeth with Group 1: 2 dimes, 2 nickels, and 9 pennies; Group 2: 2 dimes, 4 nickels, 1 penny; Group 3: 1 dime, 1 nickel, 7 pennies

36. Kendra uses the pie chart below to represent the allocation of her annual income. Her annual income is $40,000.

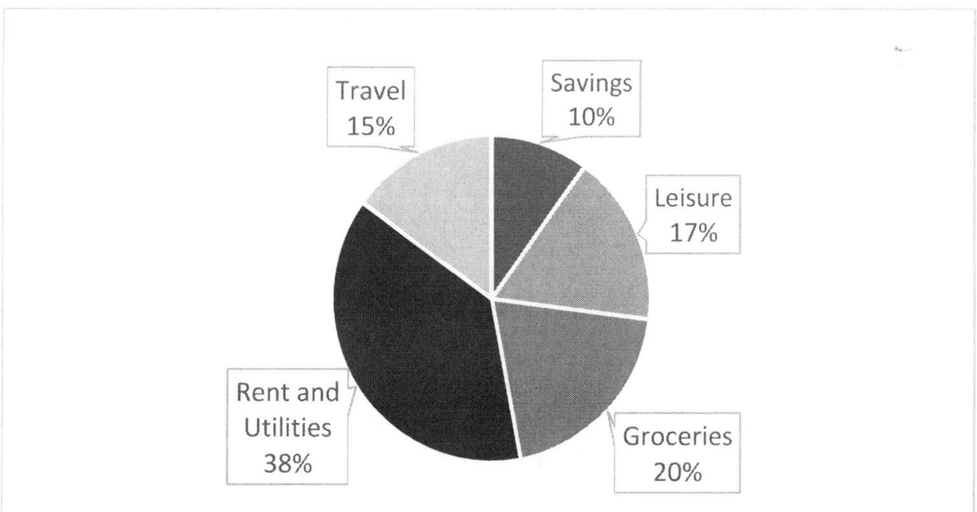

Which of the following statements is true?

a. The amount of money she spends on travel and savings is more than $11,000.
b. The amount of money she spends on rent and utilities is approximately $15,000.
c. The amount of money she spends on groceries and savings is more than $13,000.
d. The amount of money she spends on leisure is less than $5,000.

37. Which students have incorrectly listed the decimal values from least to greatest? Select all that apply.

a. Fernando: 27.09, 27.493, 27.555, 27.59, 28.01

b. Brady: 27.09, 27.493, 27.59, 27.555, 28.01

c. Trevor: 27.09, 27.493, 27.555, 27.59, 28.01

d. Dakota: 27.09, 27.59, 27.493, 27.555, 28.01

38. A teacher asks her students to find the error in this algebra problem. What is the error?

$$3x + 4x = (2^2 + 1) + 2(2)$$
$$7x = 5 + 2(2)$$
$$7x = 7(2)$$
$$7x = 14$$
$$x = 2$$

a. The student incorrectly added before multiplying.
b. The student incorrectly multiplied before adding.
c. The student incorrectly applied the exponent.
d. The student incorrectly combined like terms.

39. Kayla has a $75 budget to purchase gifts for her colleagues. She wants to buy coffee mugs and note pads. She may purchase a maximum of 30 items. Each coffee mug costs $6 and each note pad costs $3. Which of the following graphs correctly shows the possible combinations of coffee mugs and note pads that she may buy?

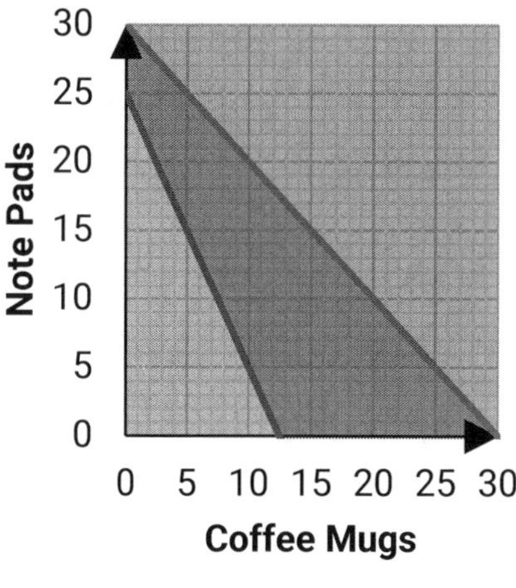

a.

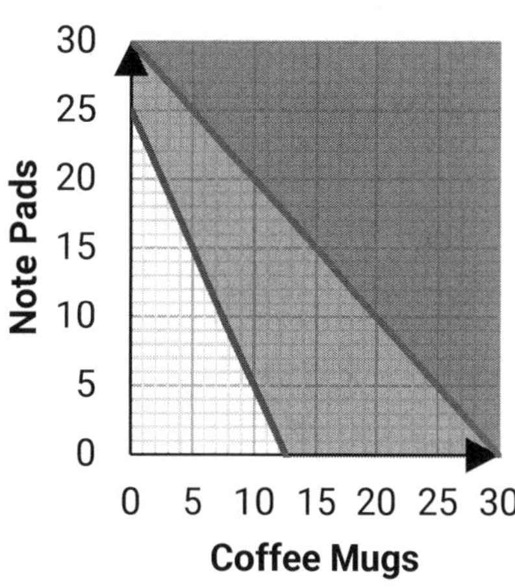

b.

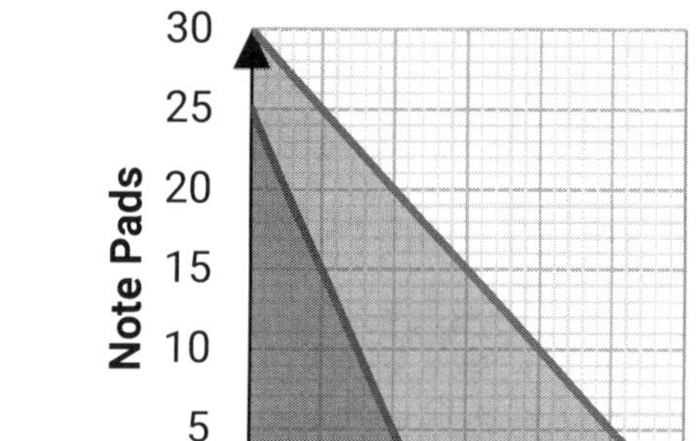

c.

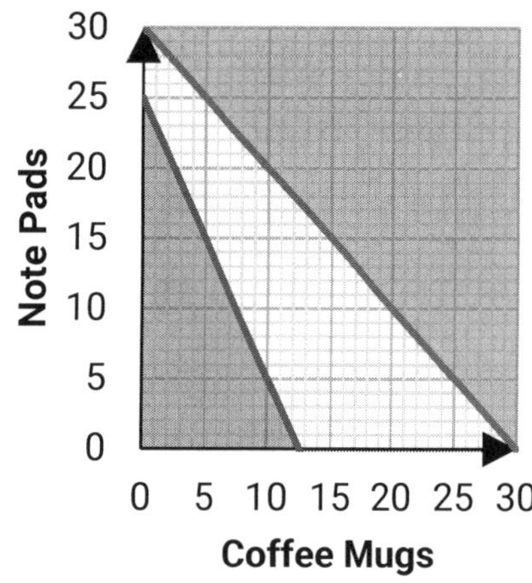

d.

40. Which of the following is NOT a model that helps students understand subtraction?

a. Take away
b. Missing addend
c. Number line
d. Adding zero

41. 400-600 word response

In this constructed response activity, you will be presented with a sample of a student's response to an assignment. You must respond by identifying a student's noteworthy strengths and their weaknesses, presenting evidence of each. Then, you must describe how you would provide an instructional intervention which builds from the student's strength to address the student's needs. Then explain how your intervention will be effective in meeting the student's needs. Your response should be between 400 and 600 words.

Exhibit 1: Background information and description of class activity

Mr. Romero recently taught a lesson on simple fractions to his second grade class. This was demonstrated by breaking a chocolate bar into fourths and by drawing the chocolate bar on the board and showing how two halves and one whole are the same. The lesson progressed into demonstrating fractions of halves, thirds, fourths, and fifths. Students were then given small round candies and were required to arrange their candies to correspond with written fractions. The students were also given Popsicle sticks to help separate out their candies into the proper groupings

Exhibit 2: Calvin's work

Key: On this assignment, students are to arrange their candies into groups based on denominator. They then would draw circles and lines representing their candies. The students would then color in those which represent the numerator.

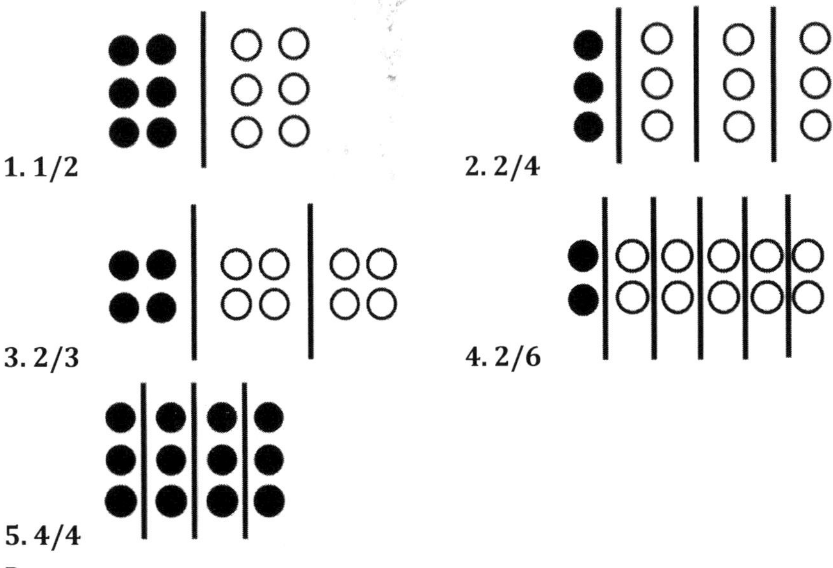

Response

Provide a response between 400 and 600 words on a separate piece of paper.

Arts and Sciences

1. In which taxonomic group are organisms MOST alike?

a. Phylum
b. Family
c. Class
d. Order

2. How does the freezing point of sea water compare to that of fresh water?

a. Sea water has a higher freezing point.
b. Sea water has a lower freezing point.
c. They are the same.
d. Sea water does not freeze.

3. Tropical climate zones are characterized by:

a. Extreme temperature variations between night and day
b. Extreme temperature variations between seasons
c. Frequent rainfall
d. All of the above

4. Which of the following is NOT true regarding the Virginia Companies?

a. One of these companies, the Virginia Company of Plymouth, made its base in North America.
b. One of these companies, the Virginia Company of London, made its base in Massachusetts.
c. One company had a charter to colonize America between the Hudson and Cape Fear rivers.
d. One company had a charter to colonize America from the Potomac River to north Maine.

5. Which of the following materials has randomly aligned dipoles?

a. A non-magnetic substance
b. An electromagnet
c. A permanent magnet
d. A horseshoe magnet

6. Which of the following is NOT true about democracy and the formation of the United States?

a. The founding fathers stated in the Constitution that the United States would be a democracy.
b. The Declaration of Independence did not dictate democracy but stated its principles.
c. The United States Constitution stipulated that government be elected by the people.
d. The United States Constitution had terms to protect some, but not all, of the people.

7. Which of the following creates a magnetic field?

a. The spinning and rotating of electrons in atoms
b. The separation of charged particles in atoms
c. The vibrational and translational motion of atoms
d. Loosely held valence electrons surrounding an atom

8. The process whereby a radioactive element releases energy slowly over a long period of time to lower its energy and become more stable is best described as which of the following?

a. Combustion
b. Fission
c. Fusion
d. Decay

9. Which of the following is true of different isotopes of the same element?

a. It has a different number of protons than its element.
b. It has a different number of electrons than its element.
c. It has a different charge as compared to its element.
d. It has a different number of neutrons than its element.

10. Which of the following was a major cause of the Great Depression of the 1930s?

a. The overproduction and underconsumption of consumer goods
b. The failure of industry to produce sufficient consumer goods
c. Underproduction and rising prices in the agricultural sector
d. The reduction of import tariffs

11. Which of the following is NOT true of careers in the art industry?

a. The majority of artists are self-employed.
b. Few artists bother earning postsecondary degrees or certificates.
c. Competition is keen for salaried jobs in the art industry.
d. Annual earnings for artists vary widely.

12. Which of the following observations provides the best evidence that sound can travel through solid objects?

a. Sound waves cannot travel through a vacuum.
b. The atoms of a solid are packed tightly together.
c. If you knock on a solid object, it makes a sound.
d. You can hear a sound on the other side of a solid wall.

13. It is snack time in your kindergarten class, and you pour two children equal amounts of water; however, one child's cup is bigger. The child with the bigger cup complains that he has less water. In terms of cognitive development, what can you determine by this complaint?

a. The child has a developmental delay because he does not understand conservation.
b. The child has not reached the concrete operational stage and does not understand conservation; this is normal for a child of this age.
c. The child is displaying a delay in intuitive processes commonly acquired during the pre-operational stage of cognitive development.
d. The child is displaying a preconceptual process that is common among this age group.

14. A country's currency increases in value on foreign currency exchange markets. What will happen as a result?

I. Exports will drop
II. Imports will rise
III. The balance of payments will rise

a. I only
b. II only
c. I and II
d. II and III

15. In a parallel circuit, there are three paths: A, B, and C. Path A has a resistance of 10 ohms, path B a resistance of 5 ohms, and path C a resistance of 2 ohms. How do the voltage and current change for each path?

a. Voltage and current are kept the same in each path.
b. Voltage is greatest in path A and current is greatest in path C.
c. Voltage is lowest in path C and current is greatest in path C.
d. Voltage is the same for each path and current is greatest in path C.

16. This organelle contains digestive enzymes that break down food and unneeded substances. They are also thought to be linked to the aging process. What part of a cell does this describe?

a. Lysosomes
b. Chromatin
c. Plastids
d. Golgi Apparatus

17. Which of the following statements is NOT correct regarding these religions under the Roman Empire?

a. The Romans generally protected the Jews until the rebellion in Judea (66 AD).
b. Julius Caesar circumvented Roman law to help Jews have freedom of worship.
c. The Druids were a religious group that the Romans ignored but also tolerated.
d. Romans viewed Christianity as a Jewish sect for its first two centuries.

18. Which division of plants produces seeds for reproduction?

a. Anthophyta
b. Lycophyta
c. Sphenophyta
d. Pterophyta

19. Which action will help dissolve a gas in a liquid if the gas and liquid are placed in a sealed container?

a. Heat the liquid.
b. Cool the liquid.
c. Shake the container.
d. Decrease the pressure on the lid.

20. What is the relative difference in frequency between these two notes?

a. 1:1
b. 2:1
c. 4:1
d. 8:1

21. What judicial system did America borrow from England?

a. Due process
b. Federal law
c. Commerce law
d. Common law

22. Which of the following have a simple life cycle, without a metamorphosis?

a. Frogs
b. Newts
c. Grasshoppers
d. Human beings

23. By correctly rendering proportion in her work, an artist can create which of the following artistic effects?

a. Emotion
b. Energy
c. Realism
d. Rhythm

24. On a topographic map, an area where the contour lines are very close together indicates which of the following?

a. A stream is present.
b. The slope is very gentle.
c. The slope is very steep.
d. The area surrounds a depression.

25. Unlike slaves, who were considered to be the property of their masters, which of the following was true regarding most indentured servants in colonial times?

a. They received wages for their labor
b. They were generally treated kindly by their employers
c. They were highly educated
d. They voluntarily entered into servitude

26. Why was US industrialization confined to the Northeast until after the Civil War?

a. Because the Civil War delayed the development of water-powered manufacturing
b. Because the Northeast had faster-running rivers than the rivers found in the South
c. Because Slater's first cotton mill with horse-drawn production lost so much money
d. Because the technical innovations for milling textiles had not as yet been invented

27. Before the Civil War, to which of the following did Southern states object?

a. An increase in Southern tobacco production
b. An increase in tariffs on Northern manufactured goods
c. An increase in western mining for gold
d. An increase in the voting rights of slaves

28. Which statement about factors related to the growth of the US economy between 1945 and 1970 is NOT correct?

a. The Baby Boom's greatly increased birth rates contributed to economic growth during this time.
b. The reduction in military spending after World War II contributed to the stronger US economy.
c. Government programs and growing affluence nearly quadrupled college enrollments in 20 years.
d. Increased mobility and bigger families caused fast suburban expansion, especially in the Sunbelt.

29. Which of these was the greatest obstacle to success for the farmers who settled on the Great Plains in the latter part of the nineteenth century?

a. The invention of barbed wire
b. Passage of the Homestead Act
c. Environmental conditions
d. The Grange movement

30. Which of the following is associated with market failure?

I. When a firm in a non-competitive industry hires labor at a lower wage
II. When the firms in a non-competitive industry create less than the efficient amount of a good or service
III. When production of a good creates negative externalities born by third parties
IV. Public goods

a. I and II only
b. I and III only
c. I, II, and III only
d. I, II, III, and IV

31. Which of the following is not an advantage angiosperms show over other types of plants?

a. Larger leaves
b. Double fertilization
c. Dormant seeds
d. Lower seed dispersal

32. The concept of checks and balances is evident in which of the following?

a. Federal judiciary appeals
b. Presidential veto
c. States' rights
d. The House and the Senate

33. Who established the precedent for the two-term limit for the US presidency?

a. Abraham Lincoln
b. Alexander Hamilton
c. George Washington
d. Thomas Jefferson

34. What is the fiber-art technique that involves condensing or matting fibers together?

a. Flocking
b. Felting
c. Macramé
d. Plaiting

35. Ms. Franklin is teaching a second-grade class a lesson on ceramics. Which of the following would be the most appropriate activity for students at this grade level?

a. Making pinch pots and coil pots
b. Throwing pots using a pottery wheel
c. Making and attaching handles to pots
d. Glazing pots using a kiln

36. The distance from the earth to the sun is equal to which of the following?

a. One astronomical unit
b. One light-year
c. One parsec
d. One arcsecond

37. What is the difference between 3/4 time and 6/8 time, by definition?

a. There is no difference.
b. 3/4 time uses three beats per measure, while 6/8 time uses six beats per measure.
c. In 3/4 time the quarter note acts as the one-beat unit, while in 6/8 time the eighth note acts as the one-beat unit.
d. 3/4 time uses a quicker tempo.

38. Which of the following is NOT true about Louis Pasteur?

a. He made the first rabies vaccine.
b. He discovered the medical use for penicillin.
c. His experiments advanced the germ theory of disease.
d. He created the first polio vaccine.

39. The purpose of an artist portfolio is MOST often to

a. demonstrate an artist's capabilities.
b. communicate past work history and education.
c. teach an artist's students.
d. include all artwork for copyright purposes.

40. The asteroid belt in our solar system is located between:

a. Earth and Mars
b. Neptune and Pluto
c. Uranus and Saturn
d. Mars and Jupiter

Answer Key and Explanations

Literacy and English Language Arts

1. B: A daze test is a specific type of cloze test. In a cloze test, words are deleted, and the reader must supply the missing words using contextual clues and vocabulary that is familiar. A daze test is a multiple-choice application of a cloze test.

2. D: When an online source is in the PDF file format or another file format that has stable pagination, MLA guidelines advise to include applicable page numbers in in-text citations because these numbers are valid and will not change. Therefore, choice D is correct. If an internet source has no pagination, as often happens, the MLA does not advise avoiding the citation, so choice A is incorrect. Rather, it advises simply making the citation without page numbers. Although a printout of an internet source will by necessity have page numbers (for the printed pages), these page numbers will be inconsistent from one printout to another, unlike PDFs. Therefore, the MLA advises not including these page numbers even if you see them, so choice B is incorrect. As already explained, there are cases where an online source will have stable pagination, and the MLA recommends including page numbers in citations of these sources, so choice C is incorrect.

3. A: Norm-referenced tests compare student scores to the average scores of a normative sample of similar students that represents the target population. Informal reading inventories (B) use graded word lists, reading passages from authentic texts, and comprehension questions to identify student reading levels, strengths, and instructional needs rather than comparing student scores to normative group scores. Curriculum-based assessments (C) test student knowledge of the specific material included in the school's curriculum rather than comparing scores. Criterion-referenced tests (D) compare student performance against pre-established criteria for mastery of specific skills, not other students' performance.

4. B: Context clues offer insight into the probable meaning of unfamiliar words.

5. B: The teacher used an informal reading inventory to gain insight into the students' abilities in a larger group setting. While some informal reading inventories, or IRIs, are administered between one teacher and one student, these inventories usually work best in a group setting. The benefit of this type of assessment is that it provides insight within the context of an entire class or large group in a short period of time. This assessment does not provide specific or generalized information about the students' progress, but rather allows the teacher to gauge her students' needs at any given point during instruction.

6. A: Phonemic awareness is the ability to recognize sounds within words, so it is a type of phonological awareness. Segmenting words and blending sounds are components of phonemic awareness. Phonological awareness includes an understanding of multiple components of spoken language. The ability to hear individual words within a vocalized stream and the ability to identify spoken syllables are types of phonological awareness.

7. B: The term *Standard English* refers to a form of English used in an English-speaking country that is reflected in dictionaries and grammar books, taught to English language learners, used in published writing, and so on. Because the rules of Standard English are adhered to mainly in edited writing, choice B is correct. Standard English actually includes a range of dialects, which is exemplified by the fact that Standard English varies between English-speaking countries, so choice A is incorrect. Standard English is not universal; different English-speaking countries have a different Standard English, so choice C is incorrect. Choice D is incorrect because edited and published writing generally adhere to some form of Standard English.

8. D: Based on a Japanese form of poetry, haiku have become popular with students and teachers alike. Reading and writing haiku helps younger students become aware of syllables and helps older students learn about subtleties of vocabulary.

9. C: These are content-specific words. Because these words are specific to paleontology, it's unlikely the students know their meanings. Without understanding what these words mean, the students would not be able to understand the content of the passage they were about to read.

10. B: Tone is the writer's attitude in a given piece of writing, as it is expressed in that writing. Voice can be thought of as the person who the reader "hears"—the particular way an individual writer expresses themselves. Choice B fills in the blanks correctly. Style (C and D) includes both of these and more; it is the effect a writer creates through purposeful use of all the elements of written language, from tone and voice to grammar and structure.

11. D: Phonemes are the smallest units of sound in words. In this activity, students are replacing one phoneme with another, which is known as phoneme substitution. Alliteration refers to a series of words in which most words begin with the same sound. Segmenting refers to breaking a word down into its individual sounds, or phonemes. Onset and rime blending involve blending the beginning sound of a word with the rest of the word.

12. C: Neologisms (from *neo-* meaning "new"), also known as "creative coinages," are new words sometimes invented by people which then become parts of our vocabulary. The word *noob* refers to a person new to a context. It was first largely used in the 1960s and 1970s to describe the new man in a military unit during the Vietnam War. Blending is another way new words come into our language; for example, *moped* is a blend of the respective first syllables of *motor* and *pedal.* Conversion, also called functional shift, changes a word's part of speech. For example, the common nouns *network, microwave,* and *fax,* along with the proper noun *Google* have all been converted to verbs in modern usage. Onomatopoeia means words that imitate associated sounds, such as *meow* and *click.*

13. C: The goal of a persuasive essay is to convince the reader that the author's position or opinion on a topic is correct. That opinion or position is called the argument. A persuasive essay argues a series of points, supported by facts and evidence.

14. C: Literacy skills are various and include a number of different sub-skills: reading fluency, comprehension, application of knowledge, listening, speaking, grammar, spelling, writing, and more. It is important for teachers to track student development for lesson design and to communicate with the student, future teachers, and parents. Therefore, it is best to keep samples of a variety of assessments, including descriptions of reading fluency, writing samples, projects, and formal assessments of grammar, spelling, and other skills. All of these skills develop simultaneously, but at different rates. Therefore, it is impossible to judge a student's literacy based only on one measure of assessment.

15. C: In Choice A, the word prince is capitalized, even though it does not have a suffix. In choice B, the word *multimedia* contains the prefix *multi-*, but no suffix. Choice C contains a word with the root *please*, which also has both a prefix and a suffix. The suffix *-ing* acts as the suffix in *displeasing*, therefore it is correctly capitalized. Choice D correctly has *bookkeeper* capitalized due to the suffix -*er* but neglects to capitalize *examined* even though it also contains a suffix. Choice C is the only correct choice available.

16. B: Consonant blend refers to a group of consonants in which each letter represents a separate sound.

17. B: Based on Charles Read's (1975) research into invented and phonetic spelling, Richard Gentry (1982, 2006, 2010) identified five phases of spelling. *Precommunicative*: Alphabetic symbols without letter-sound correspondences, complete alphabet knowledge, spelling directionality, or uppercase and lowercase letter distinctions. *Semiphonetic*: Letter-sound correspondence understanding emerges; students frequently spell words with single letters or abbreviated syllables. *Phonetic*: Not all spellings follow standard conventions, but students systematically represent all phonemes with letters. Misspellings are typically accurate in terms of articulatory placement (*e* for short *i*, *a* for short *e*, *i* for short *o*, etc.) *Transitional*: Students move from phonetic to conventional, visual spellings, informed by their growing understanding of word structure. "Higheked" for "hiked" and "egul" for "eagle" are examples of their more approximate spellings. *Correct*: Students have learned the fundamental rules of English orthography, including irregular and alternative spellings, silent consonants, prefixes and suffixes, etc., and can identify misspellings.

18. C: In one minute, a student who misreads one or less than one word per twenty words, or with 95%–100% accuracy, is at an Independent reading level. A student who misreads one or less than one word per ten words, or with 90%–95% accuracy, is at an Instructional level. A student misreading more than one word out of ten, or with less than 90% accuracy, is at a Frustration level.

19. C: The act of decoding involves first recognizing the sounds individual letters and letter groups make, and then blending the sounds to read the word. A child decoding the word *spin*, for example, would first pronounce *sp/i/n* as individual sound units. She then would repeat the sounds, smoothly blending them. Because decoding involves understanding letters and their sounds, it is sometimes known as the alphabetic principle.

20. B: Assessment is an ongoing process that involves formal testing and a host of other methods. Students are working at any given time in the school year on a multitude of skills sets, and all of these skills are interrelated and developing simultaneously at different rates. It is impossible to ever provide a "snapshot" of a student's abilities, because each student develops in a unique and complex manner. Choice "a" would only offer insight into a student's reading fluency. Choice "c" would show how a student could perform on standardized tests; however, many factors such as anxiety and test-taking speed affect those scores. Choice "d" relies on the teacher to interpret the student's strengths and weaknesses and would require an almost impossible attention to detail. Choice "b" includes both formal and informal assessments as well as giving insight into writing, vocabulary and other skill sets in a comprehensive portfolio.

21. B: According to many academic standards, second graders should be able to determine the meanings of new or unfamiliar words by comparing them to synonyms (words with similar meanings) and antonyms (words with opposite meanings). First graders are expected to use phonics (letter-sound correspondences), word roots, word suffixes, and analogies (A) to decode words for reading. It is expected of third graders to use not only known synonyms and antonyms, but additionally homophones (words sounding the same with different meanings) and homographs (words spelled the same but with different meanings) they know to discern new or unfamiliar word meanings (C). Determining word meanings by referring to word roots, prefixes, suffixes, idiomatic expressions, and familiar diacritical marks used in dictionaries (D) is expected of fourth graders.

22. C: Expository essays are any type of essay in which the writer is providing meaningful information about a topic for the purpose of informing. Most of the topics listed in the example include informational tasks, explaining the process of doing something, such as baking or juggling.

Expository essays can use various organizational schemes to help structure the information, such as by comparing and contrasting two things. An expository essay is different from an argumentative essay in that it is not trying to convince the reader of anything, but only trying to inform. Similarly, the purpose of a descriptive essay is to show detail, but not necessarily to inform about how something works.

23. D: Word recognition is required for reading fluency and is important to all readers, but it is especially so to English Language Learners and students with reading disabilities. It can be effectively taught through precisely calibrated word study instruction designed to provide readers with reading and writing strategies for successful word analysis.

24. C: The question prompt states that Ms. Baird wants to make sure her students understand certain concepts on an individual basis, rather than as a group. This scenario describes a situation in which the students support each other in creating a foundation for the activity. They help each other and are scaffolded by their teacher in determining the main ideas. However, Ms. Baird utilizes the practice of silent reading to ensure that students are practicing the skill of finding supporting evidence on an individual level. She will be able to gauge each student's comprehension levels by checking their notecards after the lesson.

25. A: Syllable types include closed, open, silent *e*, vowel team, vowel-*r*, and consonant-*le*. A closed syllable ends with a consonant, such as *cat*. Open syllables end with a vowel, such as *he*. Vowel team syllables contain two vowels working together, such as *main*. Vowel-*r* syllables such as *er* and *or* frequently occur as suffixes. Consonant-*le* syllables also typically occur as suffixes, such as *battle* or *terrible*.

26. D: CVC words, like dog, sit, and leg, are composed of a consonant, a vowel, and a consonant. To learn to read them, students must be familiar with the letters used and their sounds. A teacher can present a word like *sit* to students who also know the consonants *b/f/h/p* and ask them to create a word family of other CVC words. The students will be able to read *bit, fit, hit,* and *pit* because they are similar to the word *sit* that they have just learned.

27. B: "Pretty as a picture" is a simile (a comparison of two unlike things using the words *like* or *as*). While all similes are metaphors (but not all metaphors are similes), the phrase is best and most specifically described as a simile.

28. C: Signal words give the reader hints about the purpose of a particular passage. Some signal words are concerned with comparing/contrasting, some with cause and effect, some with temporal sequencing, some with physical location, and some with a problem and its solution. The words *since, whether,* and *accordingly* are words used when describing an outcome; outcomes have causes.

29. C: The MLA guidelines for citing sources in research papers advise that multiple authors of the same work can be cited in in-text citations by using the first author's name plus *et al*, where *et al* refers to all the other authors. However, this convention is only advised for situations where there are three or more authors, so choice C is correct. The guidelines also say that in cases where there are two or three authors, each author should be named in a serial list, either in a signal phrase or in a parenthetical reference. For example, authors Smith and Jones could be cited with "Smith and Jones note that ... (45)" or "(Smith and Jones 45)," and authors Smith, Jones, and Gray could be cited with "Smith, Jones, and Gray note that ... (45)" or simply "(Smith, Jones, and Gray 45)." Therefore, choices A, B, and D are incorrect.

30. D: Classrooms will most always consist of students at different levels of ability. The physical and psychological processes needed for reading evolve simultaneously over time and do so at different rates for each individual. No two students will match up perfectly with respect to language skills. Language skills also incorporate a variety of other processes, including speaking, listening, thinking, viewing, writing, and reading. By pairing direct instruction with various types of cognitive processes, all students receive varied instruction and will make progress. By being introduced to different types of text, students will develop skills according to their own strengths at that particular time.

31. D: Asking children to write a list provides them with a visual model that is a side-by-side comparison of the two countries. In creating that visual model, each student first has to organize his or her thoughts mentally, deciding whether each particular item under consideration is shared between both countries or is a difference between them.

32. A: Most adults can understand the relationship between oral and written language: components of oral language have representational symbols that can be written and decoded. However, most normally-developing children acquire spoken language first and begin to develop reading and writing skills as they approach school-age. Many children are first exposed to the concept of written language when an adult introduces books or other written texts. However, a child's ability to read and write develops over time and is dependent on the development of physiological processes such as hearing, sight, and fine motor skills for writing. Written language development also typically requires direct instruction. Most children must be taught to read and write and rarely learn these skills simply by observing others.

33. B: Before beginning fluency instruction, typically not before halfway through the first grade at the earliest, teachers should ensure that students have strong word recognition skills to provide the necessary foundation. Student speed and automaticity in decoding individual words are directly related to developing reading fluency (A): rapid, automatic word decoding is the precursor to fluent reading. Reading fluency not only indicates faster information processing, it also has a direct impact on comprehension (C) because the faster a student can process information, the better the student can comprehend what she reads. When a student must decode words more slowly and less automatically, both reading fluency and comprehension are decreased (D). Slow, conscious decoding does not increase comprehension by being more careful or thoughtful; instead, laborious student efforts to decode separate words for meaning divert the attention they could devote to overall comprehension if they could decode rapidly, effortlessly, and automatically.

34. A: Students are completely capable of understanding and appreciating oral traditions and written texts from other world cultures, as well as those originating from cultures in the students' own community. In fact, introducing a variety of material can increase some students' appreciation of language and literature as it enables them to learn about the world around them. Language skills emerge at a point in most children's development during which students are fascinated with learning new concepts. Introducing a variety of texts also benefits students in a classroom who belong to other cultures; these students are able to learn concepts from texts that represent their family, culture, or country of origin.

35. B: The verbs listed here all refer to taking pieces or parts of information or knowledge and bringing them together to create a whole, and to building relationships among the parts to fit new or different circumstances. Analysis is the opposite of synthesis—breaking information down into its component parts and demonstrating the relationships among those parts. An assignment for analysis would ask the student to compare, distinguish, test, categorize, examine, contrast, or analyze information. Evaluation is making judgments of information based on given criteria, confirming or supporting certain preferences, and persuading the reader. An assignment targeting evaluation would use words like evaluate, predict, appraise, conclude, score, judge, or compare.

Application is using knowledge in new contexts. The assignment would ask the student to apply, prepare, practice, use, operate, sketch, calculate, solve, or illustrate.

36. D: Targeted instruction is achieved by assessing areas needing improvement as well as areas of greatest strength for each student, and adjusting instruction to target those areas. This helps to ensure that all members of a class are receiving instruction tailored to their specific needs.

37. B: When adults or other skilled readers take time to read aloud to students, they can model (or demonstrate) what it means to read fluently. Students are still learning about grammar, spelling, decoding, comprehending, speaking, and listening. Therefore, it can be difficult for them to read aloud consistently with appropriate speed, accuracy, and inflection since there are multiple cognitive processes taking place in the student's brain. By listening to an experienced reader, students will better understand how fluent reading is intended to sound and how fluency can affect comprehension in reading or listening.

38. A: Mnemonic devices are a way to aid in memorization. The concept to be memorized is linked to a device: an easily remembered song, saying, or image. To remember the concept, one needs only to remember the device.

39. A: The student should receive instruction focused on just the areas in which he is exhibiting difficulty, which are comprehension and vocabulary. Improved vocabulary will give him greater skill at comprehending the meaning of a particular text. Strategies focused on enhancing comprehension together with a stronger vocabulary will provide the greatest help.

40. A: An introduction should move from broad, general statements about a topic to a focused and specific point regarding the topic. This point is the thesis statement. While the strongest points should come later in the body of an essay, the most attention-grabbing statements should be those in the introduction, as these will serve to engage the reader's interest in the topic and in reading the rest of the essay. Therefore, choice B is incorrect. Starting with focused and specific statements followed by broad and general statements is the opposite of how an introduction should be structured, so choice C is incorrect. Writing experts advise that the technique of beginning an essay with a dictionary definition has become overused and should therefore be avoided, so choice D is incorrect.

41. Charlie's response demonstrates that he is able to recognize key words and pull from his personal experiences to make some sense of the material he is reading. Charlie clearly employs a strategy of identifying and remembering specific content words and phrases, such as "red-light" and "run." These are likely sight words, which he has frequently come into contact with before. Making a meaningful connection with the words which he does know, he extrapolates that a young boy is learning about crossing a street safely. This is a great strategy which will help Charlie out when encountering new words later on.

Charlie is straightforward about having missed details. He indicates this by using the phrase "I think" in the fourth and sixth lines of the transcript. He probably does not have the reading recognition skills to easily notice words and phrases he probably knows well, but has not encountered in a written format. The phrase, "plays a new game," would have been a very good phrase for Charlie to notice to have a more full understanding of what the story was about. Charlie is good at recognizing some words and phrases but relies more on his context clues than trying to work through unknown words. In response, it would be effective to re-read the story with Charlie phrase by phrase and have him work his way through the words which he does not know. Making use of his verbal response, I would try to have Charlie point out the details for why he thinks the boys are talking about crossing the street. This helps Charlie learn to independently look for details which can help him understand. When he comes across words which he does not recognize, I would have him try to sound out and write them down for himself to improve vocabulary recognition and reading retention.

This strategy would be effective for addressing Charlie's reading comprehension weaknesses by helping him learn to identify the words he knows and the words which he does not know. Charlie is likely in a rush to finish this activity as he did not seem to put much effort into working through more difficult words. One of his biggest needs is to slow down and go through each word so that he does not miss important details later on. One way of helping him keep track would be to ask him step by step the five W questions to identify key facts before trying to come up with a solution. This strategy needs to be accompanied by praise when Charlie recognizes missed words and when he realizes where he missed the key points of the passage.

Mathematics

1. A: $3 + x + 3x + 3 + x = 5x + 6$ correctly shows how the combination of like terms on the left side of the equation results in the expression on the right side of the equation. $7x - 2x = 9x$ incorrectly combines like terms by adding the coefficients rather than subtracting them. $2y + 2y + 2y = 6y^3$ incorrectly adds the exponents of like terms instead of just adding the coefficients of like terms. $2.5(x + 2) = 2.5x + 2$ incorrectly distributes the 2.5 across by parentheses by neglecting to multiply the 2.5 with the last term in the expression.

2. B: The equation $y = -4x - 6$ is in slope-intercept form, $y = mx + b$, where m is the slope and b is the y-intercept. All four graphs show the correct y-intercept, −6, but only one shows the correct slope, −4. The slope of a line can be found by picking any two points (x_1, y_1) and (x_2, y_2) on the line and calculating $m = \frac{y_2 - y_1}{x_2 - x_1}$. For choice B, we can choose points $(0, -6)$ and $(-2,2)$, which gives us $m = \frac{2-(-6)}{-2-0} = -4$. None of the other graphs have a slope of −4.

3. B: A line graph is often used to show change over time. A Venn diagram shows the relationships among sets. A box-and-whisker plot displays how numeric data are distributed throughout the range. A pie chart shows the relationship of parts to a whole.

4. A: The horizontal asymptote is equal to the ratio of the coefficient of $-x$ to the coefficient of $4x$, or $-\frac{1}{4}$.

5. D: Students using cardboard manipulatives is the most learner-centered activity since it includes hands-on activities with the use of manipulatives. Watching a video and completing a worksheet are learner-centered but do not include hands-on activities. The teacher working subtraction problems on the whiteboard is teacher-centered.

6. B: Problem solving. Because an item is missing in the middle of the pattern, the process asked for cannot be counting or addition. Solving this puzzle does not involve manipulation of objects.

7. C: To solve, move the decimal left (since the scientific notation has a negative power) 2 places.

8. B: Young children often spontaneously use familiar objects to express measurements before they have learned standardized measures (e.g., "He is four teddy bears tall" or "You will be home in one *Sesame Street* [1 hour], not one *SpongeBob* [1/2 hour]). Adults should encourage rather than discourage this practice, which makes the concept of measurement understandable and relevant to them. Children will learn standard measuring units soon enough, but when they are younger there is no need to force them to learn these immediately (A). When children help with activities like grocery shopping, cooking, gardening, sewing, carpentry, etc., it will not make their participation less enjoyable to discuss measurement with them (C). Children enjoy helping parents with everyday "grown-up" tasks, and hence enjoy learning about processes involved in accomplishing them, like measuring sizes, amounts, and times. When children use their own measurement units, adults can also make use of this natural behavior by applying it themselves (D) so young children understand what they are saying about measurements.

9. A: The rectangular array represents the product of the side lengths of 4 and $(2 + 6)$.

10. C: The line through the center of the box represents the median. The median test score for classes 1 and 2 is 82.

Note that for class 1, the median is a better representation of the data than the mean. There are two low outliers, points which lie outside of two standard deviations from the mean, which bring down the average test score. In cases such as this, the mean is not the best measure of central tendency.

11. A: The student's list is correct and comprehensive: it contains all of the factors of 32. The factors of a number are all of those whole numbers that can be divided evenly into the given number. Another way of expressing this is that the factors of a number are all of the terms that can be used in a two-term multiplication problem that produces the given number. The following multiplication problems produce 32: 32×1, 16×2, and 8×4. These are the factors of 32.

12. D: This problem can be solved using the percent change formula: $\%\ change = \frac{new-old}{old} \times 100\%$. Thus, the percentage increase is represented as $\%\ change = \frac{1{,}100-800}{800} \times 100\% = 37.5\%$.

13. B, C, D: Start by ordering the race times from least to greatest. Rank the decimals by comparing each digit according to place value, from left to right: 26.06, 26.58, 26.68, 26.85, 28.05. All the statements are true except choice A. Choice A states that Baily won 1st place, which is true. However, June did not come in 2nd place. The second-place racer was Erin.

14. C: This exercise is a way to lay the foundation for measuring techniques and spatial awareness.

15. B: Rate in miles per hour can be expressed as, mph $= \frac{\text{distance in miles}}{\text{time in hours}}$. So, Zeke's driving speed on the way to Atlanta and home from Atlanta in mph can be expressed as $\frac{d}{3}$ and $\frac{d}{2}$, respectively, where d is the distance between Zeke's house and his destination. Since Zeke drove 20 mph faster on his way home, (speed home) $-$ (speed to store) $= 20$. Substitute Zeke's speeds and solve for d.

$$\frac{d}{2} - \frac{d}{3} = 20$$

$$6\left(\frac{d}{2} - \frac{d}{3} = 20\right)$$
$$3d - 2d = 120$$
$$d = 120$$

Since the distance between Zeke's house and the store in Atlanta is 120 miles, Zeke drove a total distance of 240 miles in five hours. Therefore, his average speed was $\frac{240 \text{ miles}}{5 \text{ hours}} = 48$ mph.

16. A: The probability that the dart will land in the inner circle is equal to the ratio of the area of inner circle to the area of the outer circle, or $\frac{\pi(3)^2}{\pi(6)^2}$. This reduces to $\frac{1}{4}$.

17. D: The constant of proportionality is equal to the slope. Using the points, $(2, -8)$ and $(5, -20)$, the slope may be written as $\frac{-20-(-8)}{5-2}$, which equals -4.

18. B: The volume of a sphere may be calculated using the formula $V = \frac{4}{3}\pi r^3$, where r represents the radius. Substituting 3.5 for r gives $V = \frac{4}{3}\pi(3.5)^3$, which simplifies to $V \approx 179.6 \text{ in}^3$.

19. A: The set of integers is contained within the set of rational numbers, and is hence a subset. A rational number may be written as the ratio, $\frac{a}{b}$, where a and b are integers and $b \neq 0$.

20. A: The amount to be administered may be written as $\frac{1}{12} \times \frac{34}{10}$, which equals $\frac{17}{60}$. Thus, she should administer $\frac{17}{60}$ fluid ounces of medicine.

21. C: The distance may be calculated using the distance formula, $d = \sqrt{(x_2 - x_1)^2 + (y_2 - y_1)^2}$. Substitute the given coordinates into the formula.

$$d = \sqrt{\left(4 - (-8)\right)^2 + (3 - 6)^2}$$
$$d = \sqrt{(12)^2 + (-3)^2}$$
$$d = \sqrt{144 + 9}$$
$$d = \sqrt{153}$$

Therefore, the distance between the two points is $\sqrt{153}$.

22. A: The distributive property states that $a(b + c) = ab + ac$. Though the first half of the expression contains a constant and a variable, the distributive property still applies. It is possible that the associative or the commutative law can be applied when dealing with equations like this one, but the transformation is made possible by the law of distribution.

23. D: The original cost may be represented by the equation $45 = x - 0.25x$ or $45 = 0.75x$. Dividing both sides of the equation by 0.75 gives $x = 60$.

24. D: This problem can be represented using the proportion $\frac{\textit{number of wins}}{\textit{total games}} = \frac{\textit{number of wins}}{\textit{total games}}$. If the ratio of wins to losses is 2 : 1, then the ratio of wins to total games is 2 : 3. The proportion to determine the number of wins is $\frac{x}{36} = \frac{2}{3}$.

25. B: All regular polygons have rotational symmetry. The angle of rotation is the smallest angle by which the polygon can be rotated such that it maps onto itself; any multiple of this angle will also map the polygon onto itself. The angle of rotation for a regular polygon is the angle formed between two lines drawn from consecutive vertices to the center of the polygon. Since the vertices of a regular polygon lie on a circle, for a regular polygon with n sides, the angle of rotation measures $\frac{360°}{n}$. Therefore, a square has rotational symmetry about the angle 90° and its multiples. A regular hexagon has rotational symmetry about the angle 60° and its multiples. A regular octagon has rotational symmetry about 45° and its multiples. And a regular decagon has rotational symmetry about 36° and its multiples. Since 120° is a multiple of 60°, the correct answer is a regular hexagon.

26. C: If l and w represent the length and width of the enclosed area, its perimeter is equal to $2l + 2w$; since the fence is positioned x feet from the lot's edges on each side, the perimeter of the lot is $2(l + 2x) + 2(w + 2x)$. Since the amount of money saved by fencing the smaller area is $432, and since the fencing material costs $12 per linear foot, 36 fewer feet of material are used to fence around the playground than would have been used to fence around the lot. This can be expressed as the equation:

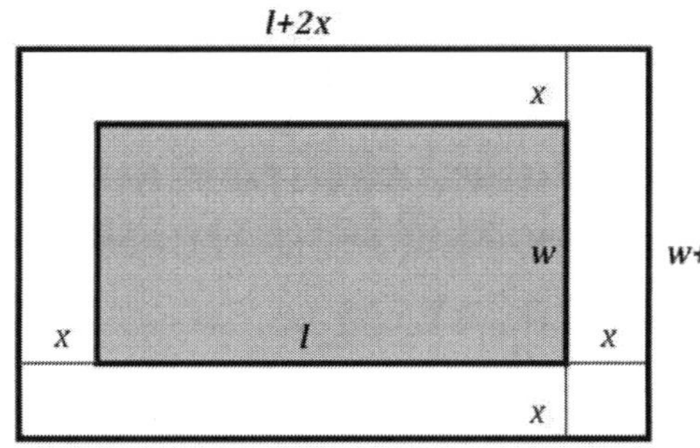

$$\begin{aligned} 2(l + 2x) + 2(w + 2x) - (2l + 2w) &= 36 \\ 2l + 4x + 2w + 4x - 2l - 2w &= 36 \\ 8x &= 36 \\ x &= 4.5 \text{ ft} \end{aligned}$$

The difference in the area of the lot and the enclosed space is 141 yd^2, which is the same as 1,269 ft^2. So, $(l + 2x)(w + 2x) - lw = 1{,}269$. Substituting 4.5 for x,

$$\begin{aligned} (l + 9)(w + 9) - lw &= 1{,}269 \\ lw + 9l + 9w + 81 - lw &= 1{,}269 \\ 9l + 9w &= 1{,}188 \\ 9(l + w) &= 1{,}188 \\ l + w &= 132 \text{ ft} \end{aligned}$$

Therefore, the perimeter of the enclosed space, $2(l + w)$, is $2(132) = 264$ ft. The cost of 264 ft of fencing is $264 \times \$12 = \$3{,}168$.

27. C: The surface area of a rectangular prism may be calculated using the formula $SA = 2lw + 2wh + 2hl$. Substituting the dimensions of 14 inches, 6 inches, and 8 inches gives $SA = 2(14)(6) + 2(6)(8) + 2(8)(14)$. Thus, the surface area is 488 square inches.

28. C: Apply the order of operations.

$$\begin{aligned} 16 \div (6 - 4)^2 &= 64 \\ 16 \div 2^2 &= 64 \\ 16 \div 4 &= 64 \\ 4 &\neq 64 \end{aligned}$$

$$\begin{aligned} 8 - 2(7 - 4) &= 18 \\ 8 - 2(3) &= 18 \\ 8 - 6 &= 18 \\ 2 &\neq 18 \end{aligned}$$

$$\begin{aligned} 2^3 \div 2 - 2(2) &= 0 \\ 8 \div 2 - 2(2) &= 0 \\ 4 - 4 &= 0 \\ 0 &= 0 \end{aligned}$$

$$\begin{aligned} 2 + 3(2^2) &= 20 \\ 2 + 3(4) &= 20 \\ 2 + 12 &= 20 \\ 14 &\neq 20 \end{aligned}$$

29. A: The repeating decimal may be converted to a fraction by writing:

$$\begin{aligned} 10x &= 7.\overline{7} \\ - \quad x &= 0.\overline{7} \end{aligned}$$

which simplifies as $10x - x = 7.\overline{7} - 0.\overline{7}$, or $9x = 7.\overline{7} - 0.\overline{7}$.

30. A: The vertical line of symmetry is represented by an equation of the form $x = a$. The horizontal line of symmetry is represented by an equation of the form $y = b$. One line of symmetry occurs at $x = -4$. The other line of symmetry occurs at $y = 6$.

31. D: The theoretical probability of tossing any particular number is $\frac{1}{6}$. Since she tosses a two $\frac{3}{12}$, or $\frac{1}{4}$ times, the experimental probability of tossing a 2 is greater than the theoretical probability. The experimental probability should grow closer to the experimental probability as she tosses the die more times.

32. D: Let $P(T)$ represent the probability of getting tails on the coin toss. We can see that $P(T) = \frac{1}{2}$. Let $P(P)$ be the chance of getting a prime number on the die. Of the possible outcomes (1 through 6), three are prime (2, 3, and 5), so $P(P) = \frac{3}{6} = \frac{1}{2}$.

Since $P(P)$ and $P(T)$ are not mutually exclusive, $P(P \text{ or } T) = P(P) + P(T) - P(P \text{ and } T)$. Because the events are independent, $P(P \text{ and } T) = P(P) \times P(T)$. Substituting the probability of each event gives $P(P \text{ or } T) = \frac{1}{2} + \frac{1}{2} - \left(\frac{1}{2} \times \frac{1}{2}\right) = \frac{1}{2} + \frac{1}{2} - \frac{1}{4} = \frac{3}{4}$.

33. A: If the digits in a number add up to a multiple of 3, it is also divisible by 3. For instance, in the number 27, $2 + 7 = 9$, which is a multiple of 3.

34. D: The numbers in this sequence progress according to a pattern. Each progressing number can be expressed by the equation $x + 2 = n$, where x is the difference between the previous two numbers and n is the number added to the previous number to yield the progressing number. For instance, the difference in 24 and 16 is 8. By adding 2 to 8, you know that you must add 10 to 24 in order to yield 34. In the next part of the sequence, $x = 10$ and $n = 12$. $34 + 12 = 46$, the next number in the sequence. Therefore, by following this pattern, you would add 16 to 60, which results in 76.

35. B: Graham has placed Group 1 with 40¢, Group 2 with 38¢, and Group 3 with 29¢. Henry has placed Group 1 with 34¢, Group 2 with 27¢, and Group 3 with 29¢. Landon has placed Group 1 with 59¢, Group 2 with 43¢, and Group 3 with 57¢. Elizabeth has placed Group 1 with 39¢, Group 2 with 41¢, and Group 3 with 22¢.

36. B: The amount she spends on rent and utilities is equal to 0.38($40,000), or $15,200, which is approximately $15,000.

37. B, D: Two of the students have correctly arranged the decimal values from least to greatest. Fernando and Trevor correctly listed the number arrangement as 27.09, 27.493, 27.555, 27.59, 28.01. Brady's list is incorrect because he lists 27.59 before 27.555. Dakota's list is incorrect because the middle three numbers are out of order. Dakota's middle three numbers are 27.59, 27.493, 27.555 and they should be 27.493, 27.555, 27.59.

38. A: In the third line of the problem, the student incorrectly added the 5 and 2 rather than multiplying 2(2). According to the order of operations, the student should multiply before adding.

39. C: The situation may be modeled by the system of inequalities $\begin{cases} 6x + 3y \leq 75 \\ x + y \leq 30 \end{cases}$ where x is the number of coffee mugs and y is the number of note pads. Some algebraic manipulation gives us the inequalities in slope-intercept form: $\begin{cases} y \leq -2x + 25 \\ y \leq -x + 30 \end{cases}$. All four choices graph these lines correctly, but only choice C correctly shades just the region that is below both lines, indicating that both conditions are met.

40. D: Adding zero. Adding zero does not assist students in understanding subtraction. Physically taking some objects away from an array of objects, working a problem with a missing addend like $7 + \_\_ = 13$ helps students learn that $13 - 7 = 6$. Moving to the left on a number line is another way of helping students understand subtraction.

41. In the skill of visually assembling fractions with counters, a student must understand multiple steps of a process. This process involves first dividing the pieces into appropriate groups based on the denominator. Then the student must draw his groupings and finally select and color in the proper number representing the numerator. In this exercise, Calvin was given twelve small candies, which he grouped appropriately in each of the five problems given to him. Calvin did very well to split the candies equally and into the proper number, which shows a strong understanding of grouping by denominator. This is shown in his splitting twelve into two groups in question 1, four groups in questions two and five, three groups in question three, and finally six groups in question four. Calvin also demonstrates that he knows that the numerator can change, as is demonstrated in question five. He does not seem to grasp this rule fully, however, as demonstrated by his always coloring only one group in questions two, three, and four. Calvin is in specific need of having numerators demonstrated thoroughly.

At this point in Calvin's understanding, he cannot proceed in further instruction in fractions without having a more clear understanding of variance possible in numerators. Instructional intervention should build from his understanding of denominators to isolate his need. This would best be approached by starting with a fraction he can recognize, such as one fourth. I would ask Calvin to identify the fraction and then show him two fourths. At this point, Calvin should independently come to the conclusion that one fourth and two fourths are differentiated by the change in colored in markers rather than by the number of groups. This form of instruction is best suited to one on one intervention, rather than as a class. Once Calvin has been capable of showing the differences between each of the fourth fractions, I would then change the denominator and have him work through similar exercises with thirds, fifths, and sixths with an increasing degree of independence.

Following the independent instruction, Calvin should be given the opportunity to make corrections to his worksheet and asked to explain what he did wrong before. This would be an adequate way of assessing Calvin's level of understanding following the instructional intervention. After proceeding through corrections, Calvin should also be given plenty of opportunity to practice over the following week. Calvin's strong skills in denominators are likely to have strong foundation, but in areas that are new or weaker, retention of new instruction may be an issue. Additional practice is supportive in building retention of new skills.

Arts and Sciences

1. B: Organisms that belong to the same taxonomic group of family are most alike. In biological taxonomy, the ranks in descending order are Domain, Kingdom, Phylum, Class, Order, Family, Genus, and Species. The ranks become more exclusive and specific as the classification descends. Phylum, class, and order are all higher than the family group. The higher the rank, the fewer requirements it takes to be a member. Two mnemonics for taxonomy are Dashing Kings Play Cards On Fat Green Stools or Dear King Philip Cuts Open Five Green Snakes.

2. B: The freezing point of sea water is lower than that of fresh water as sea water is denser. It is denser because it has more dissolved salts. The freezing point changes with salinity, pressure, and density, but can be as low as –2 °C (28.4 °F), compared with 0 °C (32 °F) for fresh water.

3. C: Tropical climate zones are characterized by frequent rainfall, especially during the monsoon season, and by moderate temperatures that vary little from season to season or between night and day. Tropical zones do experience frequent rainfall, which leads to abundant vegetation.

4. B: The Virginia Company of London was based in London, not Massachusetts. It had a charter to colonize American land between the Hudson and Cape Fear rivers. The other Virginia Company was the Virginia Company of Plymouth, which was based in the American colony of Plymouth, Massachusetts. It had a charter to colonize North America between the Potomac River and the northern boundary of Maine. Both Virginia Companies were joint-stock companies, which had often been used by England for trading with other countries.

5. A: Magnetic poles occur in pairs known as magnetic dipoles. Individual atoms can be considered magnetic dipoles due to the spin and rotation of the electrons in the atoms. When the dipoles are aligned, the material is magnetic. Choices B, C, and D are all magnetic materials. Therefore, the magnetic dipoles in these materials are not randomly aligned. Only choice A has randomly aligned dipoles.

6. A: It is not true that the founding fathers specifically stated in the Constitution that the United States would be a democracy. The founding fathers wanted the new United States to be founded on principles of liberty and equality, but they did not specifically describe these principles with the term *democracy*. Thus, the Declaration of Independence, like the Constitution after it, did not stipulate a democracy, although both did state the principles of equality and freedom. The Constitution also provided for the election of the new government, and for protection of the rights of some, but not all, of the people. Notable exceptions at the time were black people and women. Only later were laws passed to protect their rights over the years.

7. A: A magnetic field is created by a spin magnetic dipole moment and the orbital magnetic dipole moment of the electrons in atoms. Therefore, it is the spinning and rotating of electrons in atoms that creates a magnetic field. The separation of charged particles in atoms describes the nucleus and electron clouds within an atom. The vibrational and translational motion of atoms creates thermal energy. Loosely held valence electrons surrounding an atom indicates a good electrical conductor.

8. D: The process whereby a radioactive element releases energy slowly over a long period of time to lower its energy and become more stable is best described as decay. The nucleus undergoing decay, known as the parent nuclide, spontaneously releases energy most commonly through the emission of an alpha particle, a beta particle, or a gamma ray. The changed nucleus, called the daughter nuclide, is now more stable than the parent nuclide, although the daughter nuclide may undergo another decay to an even more stable nucleus. A decay chain is a series of decays of a radioactive element into different elements.

9. D: Isotopes are variations of an element that have different numbers of neutrons. The various isotopes of an element have the same numbers of protons and electrons. For example, carbon has three naturally occurring isotopes: carbon-12, carbon-13 and carbon-14 (which is radioactive). Isotopes of an element differ in mass number, which is the number of protons and neutrons added together, but have the same atomic number, or number of protons.

10. A: Along with stock market speculation, a major cause of the Great Depression was an increased supply of cars, radios, and other goods that was not matched by consumer demand. Industrial production far exceeded the population's purchasing power. Farmers were plagued by overproduction and falling prices while international trade suffered from rising tariffs.

11. B: In fact, the majority of artists hold postsecondary degrees or certificates. More than half of artists are self-employed, and competition is keen for salaried jobs in the art industry. Annual earnings for artists vary widely, according to the Bureau of Labor Statistics.

12. D: Sound cannot travel through a vacuum, though it doesn't necessarily suggest that it *can* travel through solids. Nor does the fact that atoms are packed tightly together demonstrate the fact that sound can travel through a solid. The fact that a sound is produced by knocking on a solid object also does not prove sound can pass through the object. However, if you hear a sound on the other side of a solid wall, the sound must have traveled through the wall.

13. B: The child is developing normally; typical of his age group, he is in the preoperational stage of development and has not yet mastered conservation. Conservation is the ability to use logical reasoning to determine quantity. In this case, the child thinks one glass has more water simply because the glass is smaller. As this child enters into the concrete operational stage of development, he will understand that two amounts can be equal despite the size or shape of the container they are in. However, since this skill is not yet developed, the child will continue to believe one has more. If the teacher pours the water from the bigger glass into a glass that equals the size of his classmate's, the child will have a different reaction and possibly think the two are now equal.

14. C: If a country's currency increases in value, foreigners will have to give up more of their own currency to get the original country's currency in order to buy the original country's goods and services. This will cause a drop in exports. At the same time, it will be less expensive for people in the original country to exchange their currency for foreign currencies, causing the price of imported goods to drop and the total value of imports to rise.

15. D: In a parallel circuit, the voltage is the same for all three paths. Because the resistance is different on each path but the voltage is the same, Ohm's law dictates that the current will also be different for each path. Ohm's law says that current is inversely related to resistance. Therefore, the current will be greatest in path C as it has the least resistance, 2 ohms.

16. A: A lysosome is an organelle that is thought to be linked to the aging process and contains digestive enzymes that break down food and unneeded substances. Chromatin is the structure created by DNA and various proteins in the cell nucleus during interphase and condenses to form chromosomes. Plastids are found in plants and algae. They often contain pigments and usually help make chemical compounds for the plant. The Golgi apparatus prepares macromolecules like proteins and lipids for transport.

17. C: The Druids were neither ignored nor tolerated by the Romans. Conversely, the Druids were viewed as "non-Roman" and therefore were suppressed. Augustus (63 BC–14 AD) forbade Romans to practice Druid rites. According to Pliny, the Senate under Tiberius (42 BC–37 AD) issued a decree suppressing Druids, and in 54 AD, Claudius outlawed Druid rites entirely. It is correct that the Romans generally protected the Jews up until the rebellion in Judea in 66 AD. In fact, Julius Caesar circumvented the Roman laws against "secret societies" by designating Jewish synagogues as "colleges," which in essence permitted Jews to have freedom of worship. After the rebellion in Judea, according to Suetonius, the Emperor Claudius appeared to have expelled all Jews, probably including early Christians, from Rome. The Roman Empire viewed Christianity as a Jewish sect, which was how Christianity began, for 200 years following its emergence. It is also correct that according to Tacitus, when much of the public saw the Emperor Nero as responsible for the Great Fire of Rome in 64 AD, Nero blamed the Christians for the fire in order to deflect guilt from himself. Following their persecution of Jews, the Roman Empire would continue to persecute Christians for the next two centuries.

18. A: Anthophyta is a division of plants that produces seeds as part of reproduction. Anthophyta are also known as the group that contains flowering plants. It is the largest and most diverse grouping of plants and includes many food, clothing, and medicinal uses for humans. Grains, beans, nuts, fruits, vegetables, spices, tea, coffee, chocolate, cotton, linen, and aspirin are all derived from plants from anthophyta. Lycophyta is a small group of plants including club mosses and scale trees. Sphenophyta contains about thirty species including horsetails, foxtails, or scouring rushes. Pterophyta contains non-seed plants like ferns. Lycophyta, sphenophyta, and pterophyta all use spores to reproduce sexually.

19. B: If a gas and a liquid are placed in a sealed container, cooling the liquid will help dissolve the gas into the liquid. Gases have higher solubility in liquids at lower temperatures. At higher temperatures, the gas molecules will have more kinetic energy and will have enough energy to overcome intermolecular interactions with the liquid solvent and leave the solution. This also explains why heating the liquid is incorrect. Shaking the container is also incorrect as this would give the gas energy to escape. Decreasing the pressure on the lid may or may not significantly affect the pressure inside the vessel depending on the nature of the vessel, but decreasing the pressure inside the vessel would decrease the solubility of the gas in the liquid.

20. B: 2:1. Both notes are G, separated by one octave. An octave is the interval between two notes, where the higher note's frequency is exactly twice that of the lower. Choice A, 1:1, is incorrect, because obviously the notes are not the same. One is higher than the other and therefore has a higher frequency. Choices C and D are both incorrect, since a frequency ratio of 4:1 or 8:1 refers to differences of two and three octaves, respectively.

21. D: America is a common law country because English common law was adopted in all states except Louisiana. Common law is based on precedent and changes over time. Each state develops its own common laws.

22. D: Human beings, like other mammals, birds, fish, reptiles, and spiders, have simple life cycles in that they are either born live or hatched from eggs, and then grow to adulthood. Frogs (A), newts (B), and grasshoppers (C) undergo metamorphoses wherein their forms change. Frogs and newts are amphibians; they begin life underwater, breathing through gills, but breathe through lungs by adulthood and move from the water to live on the land. Grasshoppers hatch from eggs into larvae, wormlike juvenile forms that do most of the feeding they need; then they progress to adulthood.

23. C: By correctly rendering proportion in her work, an artist can achieve a sense of realism. Correctly rendering proportion involves depicting the size relationships within and among objects as they are actually perceived by the human eye. For example, objects in the foreground of a painting should generally be larger than objects in the background (even if they are smaller in real life) since this is how the human eye perceives them.

24. C: On a topographic map, an area where the contour lines are very close together indicates that the slope is very steep. Lines very far apart would indicate a more gradual change in elevation. Contour lines help represent the actual shape of the Earth's surface features and geographic landmarks like rivers, lakes, and vegetation. Topographic maps also show man-made features such as roads, dams, and major buildings. They are based on aerial photography, and the quadrangle maps are produced in various scales. The 7.5-minute quadrangle is very common and provides a 1:24,000 scale, where 1 inch represents 2,000 feet.

25. D: Indentured servants agreed to work for a set period of time in exchange for transportation to the New World and such basic necessities as food and shelter. They did not receive wages and were generally not highly-educated people. Employers often viewed indentured servants with scorn and treated them as harshly as they treated slaves.

26. B: US industrialization was confined to the Northeast until after the Civil War because the Northeast had faster-running rivers than the South. The earliest American factories used horse-drawn machines. When waterpower was developed and proved superior, the Northeast's faster rivers were more suited to water-powered mills than the South's slower rivers. The war did not delay the development of waterpower. Waterpower was developed before the Civil War in the late 1790s. Steam power, a more efficient alternative to waterpower, was developed after the Civil War and eventually replaced waterpower. With steam-powered engines, industry could spread to the South, since steam engines did not depend on rapidly running water like water-powered engines. While British emigré Samuel Slater's first cotton mill using horse-drawn production did lose a lot of money, this was not a reason for industrial delay. In fact, Slater's Beverly Cotton Manufactory in Massachusetts, the first American cotton mill, in spite of its financial problems, was successful in both its volume of cotton production and in developing the water-powered technology that ultimately would succeed the horse-drawn method. Slater's second cotton mill in Pawtucket, Rhode Island, was water-powered. Industrial delay was not because milling technology had not yet been invented. Slater learned of new textile manufacturing techniques as a youth in England, and he brought this knowledge to America in 1789.

27. B: Southern states provided raw materials that were manufactured into commodities in Northern states. Southerners resented paying taxes to Northern states for these products (textiles, furniture, etc.).

28. B: There was not a reduction in military spending after the war. Although the manufacturing demand for war supplies and the size of the military decreased, the government had increased military spending from $10 billion in 1947 to more than $50 billion by 1953—a more than fivefold increase. This increase strengthened the American economy. Other factors contributing to the strengthened economy included the significantly higher birth rates during the Baby Boom from 1946 to 1957, which stimulated the growth of the building and automotive industries by increased demand. Government programs, such as the GI Bill (the Servicemen's Readjustment Act of 1944), other veterans' benefits, and the National Defense Education Act all encouraged college enrollments, which increased by nearly four times. Additionally, larger families, increased mobility and low-interest loans offered to veterans led to suburban development and growth as well as increased home construction. Improvements in public health were also results of the new affluence; the rate of infant deaths decreased significantly, and as a result, from 1946–1957, the American life span rose from 67 to 71 years. Moreover, Dr. Jonas Salk developed the polio vaccine in 1955, which virtually wiped out poliomyelitis, preventing many deaths and disabilities in children.

29. C: Nature imposed great hardships on farmers. Drought, wind, fires, blizzards, and subzero temperatures made life on the plains very difficult and dangerous. The invention of barbed wire in 1874 allowed farmers to keep livestock from damaging their crops. The Homestead Act of 1862 encouraged settlement of the west and made land available to some 600,000 homesteaders. Founded in 1867, the Grange united farmers in their effort to regulate storage and shipping costs and generally protect their own interests.

30. D: A market failure is any situation in which the production of a good or service is not efficient. In the cases listed, non-competitive markets allow for the underpayment of labor and the underproduction of a good or service; externalities are negative consequences assumed by parties not involved in a transaction; and public goods are an example of a good the market will not produce at all, or at efficient levels.

31. D: Lower seed dispersal is not an advantage that angiosperms show over other types of plants. Gymnosperms, for example, have plentiful amounts of pollen, but it does not always hit its mark. Angiosperms are the most recently evolved plant division and contain at least 260,000 extant species. They are very diverse and occupy many habitats. Many other species in other plant divisions do not have true leaves. Gymnosperms have modified leaves in the form of needles. Double fertilization refers to how one sperm cell fuses with an ovule, forming the zygote. The second sperm forms into a triploid endosperm that provides energy for the embryo.

32. B: The President may veto legislation passed by Congress. The executive branch has this "check" on the legislative branch.

33. C: George Washington served 2 four-year terms as president. This interval of time was not specified in the Constitution, but future presidents followed suit (until FDR).

34. B: The fiber art technique that involves condensing, or matting, fibers together is called felting. Flocking involves applying small fibers to the surface of a fabric to enhance its texture. Macramé fabric is produced by knotting yarns or threads. Plaiting (also known as braiding) involves intertwining multiple threads in a consistent pattern.

35. A: The most appropriate activity for students at this grade level would be making pinch pots and coil pots. Pinch pots are formed by creating a depression in the center of a ball of clay and smoothing the sides. Coil pots are formed by creating a long, thin length of clay and coiling it to form a pot. Unlike making and attaching handles to pots or throwing pots using a pottery wheel, creating this type of object with clay is appropriate given the fine motor skills and technical sophistication of second graders. The art teacher could model glazing pots using a kiln, but this activity would be too dangerous for young students to attempt on their own.

36. A: The average distance from the earth to the sun is equal to one astronomical unit (AU). An AU is equal to 93 million miles and is far smaller than a light-year or a parsec. A light-year is defined as the distance light can travel in a vacuum in one year, and is equal to roughly 63,241 AU. A parsec is the parallax of one arcsecond and is equal to 2.0626×10^5 astronomical units.

37. C: In 3/4 time, the quarter note is selected as the one beat unit, while in 6/8 time the eighth note is used. Essentially, 6/8 time is the same as the six-note form of 3/4. The only difference is that the eighth note is used as the one-beat unit.

38. D: French chemist Louis Pasteur (1822–1895), considered one of the founders of bacteriology, developed a process of heating and cooling food products like milk and wine that reduces the number of pathogenic microbes to a level that will not cause sickness when ingested. This process is named pasteurization after him. Pasteur also made the first vaccines against both rabies and anthrax. All three of these accomplishments were incredible breakthroughs in preventing fatal diseases. Pasteur's experiments advanced the germ theory of disease, which when first proposed, met strong resistance from those who did not believe microorganisms cause sickness. His work supported its acceptance and colleague Robert Koch's proof of it in 1890. However, Pasteur did not create the first polio vaccine.

39. A: Artists will often use portfolios to demonstrate their capabilities. Portfolios are not designed to communicate past work history or education and are rarely used for teaching purposes. The intention of a portfolio is not to showcase an artist's entire body of work, but instead to highlight select pieces. A portfolio is also not intended to lay claim to copyright privileges.

40. D: The asteroid belt in our solar system is located between Mars and Jupiter. The asteroid belt is populated by asteroids and dwarf planets that are distributed thinly enough that spacecraft can pass through the belt with relative ease.